Perfect Health

in 20 weeks

Perfect Health
in 20 weeks

Amar Chandel

KONARK PUBLISHERS PVT LTD

KONARK PUBLISHERS PVT LTD
206, First Floor, Peacock Lane,
Shahpur Jat, NEW DELHI - 110 049 (INDIA)
Ph.: (011) 41055065, 65254972
E-mail: konarkpublishers@hotmail.com

Copyright © Amar Chandel, 2010

ISBN No: 81-220-0781-3

All rights reserved. No part of this book may be reproduced or utilised in any form or by any means, electronic or mechanical, including photocopying, recording, or by any information storage and retrieval system, without prior permission in writing from the publishers.

Edited by
Sunita Pant Bansal

Typeset & Design by
SPB Enterprises Pvt. Ltd.
www.spbenterprises.net.in

Printed at
Excel Printers Pvt. Ltd. C-205, Naraina Phase I New Delhi - 110028

Foreword

According to the ancient traditions of India, good health forms the basis of all our worldly performances. On the other hand, ill health or disease not only hampers our actions and achievements, but also destroys the well-being and the life itself.

The idea of health put forth by the Vedic beliefs is so perfect and comprehensive that it not only surpasses the proverb 'Health is wealth,' but in addition, establishes an understanding of a positive and accomplished life.

It is well known that diseases have two causes. First, they can arise from physical and biological reasons; and second, our faulty lifestyle, which in the present era is largely responsible for far more number of ailments. The total conditioning of the body includes the physical, mental and spiritual aspects, which requires a holistic approach to the treatment.

I have known Amar Chandel for many years and his knowledge and experience in holistic ways of healing is remarkable. He has well conceived the ideas of our ancient masters regarding adopting a balanced lifestyle, supported by yoga and meditation. It is due to his hard work and deep study of the subject, that his training courses imparting good health prescriptions are equally successful in India and abroad.

The present work is a praiseworthy effort to convey this intricate subject in a simple, lucid and comprehensive manner.

Dr. R. Vatsyayan
Chikitsak Guru - Rashtriya Ayurveda Vidyapeeth
Member - Medicinal Plants Board, Chandigarh (U.T)
Former Member - Governing Body, Central Council for
Research in Ayurveda and Siddha (CCRAS)
Ludhiana
India

Introduction

Welcome to the community that treats one's body as a holy temple to be kept free from all polluting influences and to be revered as God's greatest and irreplaceable gift to us.

Congratulations on your decision to take charge of your health, happiness and harmony. These are indeed our responsibilities, and not that of any outside agencies, like hospitals or doctors.

Most people suffer from one or more of the following three problems: (1) Emotional difficulties like depression or aggression, (2) Physical ailments and/or (3) Obesity or excess weight.

Even though these three problems may appear unrelated, they are actually all inter-connected. The saving grace is that if you decide to set right one of them, the others, too, are also taken care of. In other words, if you begin to work on removing your illness, the emotional problems are also solved to a large extent. Similarly, resolving emotional problems may also free you from physical ailments.

Regaining your health, happiness and shedding your weight is not only a physical endeavour, but also a psychological battle. You have to convince yourself of the following:

(a) You have to fight this war,
(b) You can win it, and
(c) You are more than equal to this task.

You see, the human body is a machine like any other. The only difference is, that it is a million times more efficient and complicated than any man-made machine. Now, to run any machine efficiently, we have to follow certain rules. Let us take the example of a car. To keep the car in a perfect condition, one has to ensure that its engine is well tuned and there is petrol in the tank, sufficient air in the tyres and sufficient water in the radiator. Similarly, to keep the human body in perfect health, we have to take care of the following essential requirements:

1. Food
2. Water
3. Air or breathing
4. Physical movement or exercise
5. Rest
6. Sleep
7. Positive attitude
8. Right social interaction
9. Common sense (everything from brushing your teeth and combing your hair)

If any of these parameters go wrong, our body suffers. In fact this impacts not only our body, but our emotions and our mind also go haywire.

These are all mandatory requirements. This means that even if you are doing very well in three or four of the aforementioned fields, you cannot afford to ignore the other fields. Think of these as subjects of a matriculation examination. Even if you attain a 'distinction' in some subjects but fail in one or two of the others, you will get to take those examinations again and lose precious time. The consequences can be horrible. Some of them are given below.

1. Unease

2. Disease
3. Weight increase
4. Lack of energy
5. Bad mood (aggression or depression)
6. Premature ageing
7. Shorter life

Reading this book and following the advice given herein, will ensure that you get at least passing marks in ALL subjects, although I would be satisfied only if you get 100 out of 100 in each subject and regain every ounce of health that Nature had intended you to have in the first place.

Just as you procure a lot of equipment and do a lot of practice before attempting to climb a mountain, you should prepare yourself similarly for this endeavour.

All the best!

Amar Chandel

Contents

Foreword		v
Introduction		vii
Week 1:	Setting the weight target, maintaining a food diary & starting a physical regimen	1
Week 2:	Why do we eat, what happens to what we eat & how to eat properly	5
Week 3:	Importance of chewing well	12
Week 4:	Eating consciously to understand the amount of food required by our body	18
Week 5:	Understanding the digestive system & the importance of exercise	25
Week 6:	Banishing refined flour from the diet	35
Week 7:	Improving the nutritive value of the flour in the diet & understanding basic yoga	41
Week 8:	Banishing milk & its products from the diet & learning some ankle exercises	48
Week 9:	Importance of water for our system & knee and hip exercises	55
Week 10:	The acid-alkali balance of our body & waist and shoulder exercises	62
Week 11:	Importance of the time gap between meals & neck exercises	69
Week 12:	Banishing sugar from the diet & more on neck care	77

Week 13:	Banishing fat from the diet & learning shoulder exercises	88
Week 14:	Resting the system for a day in a week & eye exercises	95
Week 15:	Learning Pranayam & arm exercises	102
Week 16:	Some rules about foods linked to the time of their ingestion & more arm exercises	109
Week 17:	Importance of sleep & breathing exercises	116
Week 18:	General body exercises	123
Week 19:	Cleansing programme for the body	130
Week 20:	Simple meditation	138

Week 1

The first thing I want you to do is to already start believing that you are at your ideal weight and in a disease-free condition (physically and emotionally). Only then will your subconscious mind start being a helper instead of a hindrance. By now you know your ideal weight. Write down this figure on small stickers and paste it at a dozen places, or at least, where you are going to see it daily a number of times. For instance, it must be on your bathroom mirror, car dashboard and inside your purse. Don't worry about what people will think. Most of them will not even notice it. Those who do and are too inquisitive, can be fobbed off by telling them it is a reminder to yourself that you have to make this much money. Any such story will do!

Don't underestimate the power of this small step. Miracles are performed through such small steps. So just go ahead and do it. Suppose your ideal weight is 70 kg. The stickers with '70' written on them should be everywhere in your house. Do not be disillusioned even if you have to shed 40 kilograms. Many others have done this before you. At least, don't be stingy while dreaming. Think big and your wishes will come true. I say this sincerely.

Another similar preparation you have to do, is to locate a cheerful photograph of yourself in full view when your weight was just right. Maybe you were lean and wiry when you were in school or college. Or was it at the time of your wedding? Dig out that photo and get some 20 copies of it made. Since photo printing is done through computers these days, getting such copies is very easy. Even if such an old photo is in a group, your photo can be easily singled out. This photo must also be displayed at many places as a reminder to yourself that you were *that* thin once. If you could be like you were at that time, there is no reason why you cannot be the same today.

Perhaps you were always a little on the heavy side? Nothing to worry about! Just pick up the photo of your favourite hero/heroine or model. There is just no reason why you cannot be like him/her. I guarantee you can. I just want you to go along with me. Come on. Give it your best shot.

The third thing you have to do is to start writing a diet diary. Put the date on top of the page. Whenever you drink or eat anything, note it down in the diary along with the time at which it was consumed and also the quantity. Even if you take a glass of water, it has to be jotted down. So from morning till night, you have to keep a meticulous record of what you consume. It may seem difficult to begin with, but soon you will get the hang of it.

Even when you go out and cannot carry your diary along, you must jot down your intake on a piece of paper and later transfer it to the diary. Don't cheat on this job! You will only be fooling yourself. Whatever goes past your lips has a profound bearing not only on your health but also on your emotions. So please keep a comprehensive record of whatever you consume. The full benefit of this habit will manifest itself only later.

Most of the people one meets say that they are very light eaters. They are not liars. It is a human habit to forget most of what we eat. Some day, realisation will dawn on you that you had been nibbling far more than what you should have.

There is another advantage. You will shirk from eating a few items merely because you know that you will have to also enter them in your diary.

Even when you are certain that nobody else is going to read your diary, you may have this lurking fear that someone will peep into it some day, and laugh at you for being the glutton that you are.

There is another thing. Along with the food, time and quantity, also jot down the mood in which you ate something. For instance, were you tense at that time? Or sad? Or just hard-pressed for time? This description of mood will help you at a later stage. For the time being, just do it on my prodding.

And you are also to spend some good money on a nice pair of walking shoes. You see, most of us just do not get into the habit of walking, which is absolutely essential for keeping in good health. There are a million excuses for not hitting the trail. Being pressed for time; the weather not being right and your health being iffy are some of the more popular ones.

Even those who bring themselves to start walking after all, go out in improper shoes. Some use party shoes, some would even wear sandals. The result is that they tire easily or develop foot sores. Their enthusiasm for walking wanes and now they also have a *genuine* reason not to go out for a walk.

To get rid of this excuse, you must have a good pair of sneakers which you must religiously wear every morning so that you are up and about. The best that you can afford would be right. And if you can manage it, why don't you keep another pair right there in the boot of your car? That way, you can hit the trail, whenever you have a couple of minutes to spare, even when you are in the market. Let me tell you right away that, by and by, you have to increase your walk to at least 10,000 steps every day. That will come much later, but it is best that you start preparing for the day right away.

One small precaution is to be taken. Even if you have a good pair of shoes, which is *as good as new*, discard it if it is more than six months old or has served you for more than 200 km. Its exterior may be in good

shape but the interior has gone uneven and will hurt your feet at odd places. The money you spend on a new pair will be far less than the complications that the old one will create for your feet.

In your diary, also note down what – walk, jog, yoga, gym or exercise – you did on that particular day. Aim to do your basic physical regimen at least five days a week.

So, complete these basic formalities and you are ready to proceed towards the goal of a healthy, well-toned body. Best of luck!

Week 2

Why do we eat food at all? Answer this simple question in a simple manner. Think of the most obvious as well as most outlandish reasons. Well, listed below, are some of the main reasons because of which we eat food.

1. To gain energy
2. To satiate hunger
3. To satisfy our taste buds
4. To fulfil social obligations
5. Out of boredom
6. Comfort eating
7. Out of habit
8. As an addiction

Now let us discuss all these eight reasons one by one in some detail.

1. To gain energy

The first and foremost reason is that food is essential for running our body. It is, what fuel is to a car. The body needs it to grow, survive and repair itself. There is no tablet or syrup, so far, which can replace food. So much so, that when astronauts go to space, their food supply has to be sent from the Earth, even though it has been estimated that sending one pound of material to space costs as much as 100,000 US dollars. You can well imagine how much providing food for the astronauts costs! But since there is no alternative, the cost just has to be borne. To that extent, food is unavoidable for us.

2. To satiate hunger

The second reason for eating is that if we do not eat, we suffer from hunger pangs. These can be almost unbearable for most of us. In fact, many household discords begin because the lady of the house was late in providing lunch to the hungry husband. Well, the fact of the matter is that a 10-minute delay in eating does not kill anybody, but when one is hungry, even one minute seems like eternity.

This basic urge was made by Nature with a very specific reason. It wanted to make sure that even if someone was very busy, he or she would not forget to eat. Supposing this instinct wasn't there and someone did forget to get his regular quota of food, the body organs would be badly affected. So, the basic purpose of hunger is to ensure that no one goes without food for too long.

3. To satisfy our taste buds

The third and most dangerous reason for eating is the pampering of taste buds. We eat even when we are neither hungry nor in need of energy. We know we should not eat, but we lose control when we come across items that are our favourites. I wonder if it has ever happened to you, but millions of people report that at times, when going home in the evening, they feel that they had eaten too much during the office hours and they would skip dinner now. They reach home and ask their wife: "What do we have for dinner tonight?" If she says it is *lauki ki sabzi* (a bottle-gourd curry) or some other equally *unpalatable* dish, their resolve 'not to eat' remains. But supposing she has cooked their favourite *paneer pasanda* (cottage-cheese curry) or soufflé, they change their mind. So strong is the pull of taste buds.

4. To fulfil social obligations

Social eating is equally compelling. I go to your house or you come to mine. Both of us will end up eating quite a lot of food despite knowing that we must not. Not joining in partaking of food is considered bad manners.

By the way, have you noticed that we have converted every social function into an occasion for eating? Whether it is childbirth or birthday or marriage, no function is complete without a lavish meal. We have a feast even when someone has died or when we are observing the 10th or 12th day of the cremation ceremony, or the religious event after a year known as *barsi*, or the first death anniversary!

5. Out of boredom
Food has also come to be treated as a device to while away time. You are watching TV and somebody brings a packet of popcorn. Hey Presto! It is gone because you have nothing better to do!

6. Comfort eating
It is a confirmed fact that we also eat to compensate for many emotional difficulties that we may be having. Food becomes a substitute for the emotional needs that are left unfulfilled.

7. Out of habit
Food is an acquired habit. A north Indian may have eaten tons of *dosas*, *tikkis*, *chat* and what not; he will still feel hungry if he does not get his daily fill of *roti-dal*. A South Indian will similarly feel unhappy without his *sambhar-dosa* or curd-rice.

8. As an addiction
Food is an addiction, too. We know we have diabetes or indigestion or any other such ailment, but we still cannot stop eating the things that we must not.

Amidst all these reasons, real or imaginary, what is clear is that the basic purpose for eating is for sustenance. All others are only psychological reasons.

Even hunger has been specifically designed by Nature lest we get so busy that we forget to eat food. After all, we do forget so many other chores when pressed for time, don't we?

The problem is that whatever we eat over and above our energy requirements, it does not easily pass out of the body. It simply sits there for a long time, causing us numerous problems like:

a) Unease
b) Disease
c) Weight increase
d) Lack of energy
e) Bad mood (aggression or depression)
f) Premature ageing
g) Shorter life

In most cases, the total intake of food is several times more than the actual need. All this excess baggage is what has killed a large number of people and has affected the life of ten times more people. *We have to eat food as a medicine, only to gain energy, at least during the next 20 weeks.* That is exactly what Hippocrates (*ca.* 460 BC – *ca.* 370 BC, considered the father of medicine, in whose name doctors still take the Hippocratic oath on getting their medical degree), had advised: "Let thy food be thy medicine." Sadly, we have forgotten what the Greek legend had told us.

So, the body needs energy, not food. This energy conversion takes place in our digestive system. Take this as our refinery plant where the crude oil extracted from the earth is cleaned into petrol, diesel and kerosene and so on. Refineries are located far, far away from petrol outlets.

This *refinery* in human beings happens to be right inside the body but it is hermetically sealed from the rest of the body and the food is supposed to go in here only and nowhere else.

Once the food is converted into energy, the energy is supplied from here to the rest of the body while the waste material is expelled from the system.

While this actual conversion takes place in the small intestine, the process of digestion begins much before that. The mandatory condition of the small intestine for converting food into energy is that it should be in liquid (chyme) form. Only then can chyme be transformed into energy by the complex machinery that is the small intestine. That means that the food that is poured from the stomach into the small intestine has to be of the consistency of cream soup.

We think that our stomach will perform this job. The problem is that the stomach to which we send food is only a churner, not a grinder. It cannot break down large pieces of food, which never get converted into energy; instead they cause obesity, unease and disease as mentioned earlier.

The only place where food can be converted into liquid form is your mouth, which has as many as 32 grinders, called teeth, to do the job. We have been telling our children to "chew your food" all our lives, but we never did so ourselves, for the simple reason that we never knew how important it was to do so.

So from now on, use the number of teeth (32) as a reminder that you have to masticate every morsel 32 times.

There are certain soft food items like pastries and *ras malai* (milk-based pudding) which simply melt in the mouth and it is next to impossible to keep them from slipping into the gullet while you count up to 32, which is a good 20 seconds. They may go down by the time you are counting up to five or six. The trick lies in not taking the next bite till the count of 32 is complete. There is a very specific reason for it.

You see, to digest the food eaten by us, our digestive system has to mix several chemicals in it. Some of them are made only in the mouth. Our saliva is a full-fledged chemical factory whose produce has to go to the stomach along with the food.

It is estimated that each day, nearly three litres of saliva must be produced and sent in. But because we eat hurriedly, this much of supply is never sent in. *The actual supply is no more than one-quarter of a litre!* Imagine a household, which needs three litres of milk every day, but gets only 250 ml. How will the family be fed? That is exactly what happens to our body. We think we are eating healthy food, but since this healthy food is not supplemented by enough saliva, it goes waste. In place of making us healthy, this food makes us fat, weak and sick.

So, when we chew our food, we are not only ensuring that it turns into liquid before it goes into the stomach, we are also mixing sufficient quantity of saliva in it and thus giving it the benefit of the full quota of chemicals which are not produced anywhere else in the body.

God has made a wonderful arrangement to enhance this supply to the maximum extent possible. Even when you have not started eating, and only smell the food being readied for you, your mouth starts watering (*munh mein paani aa gaya*, as they say). This way some saliva reaches the system even before the food has been despatched.

But this much of it is just not enough. So, you spend more and more time with every bite. Enjoy its taste, flavour, texture and consistency. Take it as a bounty from Mother Nature. In fact, enjoy it as if it is the last bite you are ever going to take. You will be amazed how much enjoyment and satisfaction every morsel will give you.

It is strange, that whatever else we love we spend time with it. You enjoy visiting exotic places. You want to spend as much time there as possible. You love to watch movies. You wish the film never ends. But, ironically, we are all food lovers and yet are always in a rush to finish the job by eating as quickly as possible!

We think it is all due to pressure of time, and lack, thereof. Actually, the roots of the habit go far deeper than that. The human beings acquired it when they were living in jungles, food was scarce and they had to struggle to fill their belly. Like animals, there was a battle for every morsel

and only he had his fill, the one who could gobble up food in a hurry!

That period of famine is long over; we are now civilised, but the old habit remains. There is a need to break away from it forcefully. Please remind yourself that there has been no instance in the past, in many years – rather decades – in your life that while you were eating your food slowly, somebody grabbed it and ran away! So, there is no point hurrying. Slow down and enjoy it as much as you can. Only then can you get the full benefit from it.

Chew well, live well!

Week 3

So, how is your Operation *Chew Well* going? If you are a typical starter, I am sure your jaws must be aching. Don't worry. The pain will go away soon enough.

You must be feeling bored with all that seemingly endless munching, but you will agree that this dullness is any day better than the scores of problems one has to face if one eats too fast.

Let us discuss just a few of them. That will also answer a niggling question that might have cropped up in your mind: what happens to those who eat too quickly? After all, that is how most of us eat food. And they still seem to be doing pretty well, don't they?

It is not as if the food does not get digested at all. It's just that the task, which would have been performed in a few seconds in due course by your mouth, now has to be handled by your abdomen. After all, they comprise a team called the *digestive system* and if one falls back, another organ selflessly takes over. However, it is an additional burden for the latter and the strain shows. And how!

You see, the abdomen knows only one way of digesting food: by adding gastric juices, mainly acid, to it. After all, it is a churner and not a grinder. So, it steps up the production of acid – and a concentrated one, at that

– to tackle the unmanageably big chunks of food. That is akin to us cleaning a washbasin with water first, then adding some soap to the water and then going in for a toilet cleaner. But if the stains are really stubborn, we take a bottle of acid, pour it on the stains and let it sit there for a few hours. Then with a piece of wood or some other such non-corrosive material, we clean up the stains.

Big portions of food particles are taken care of in the same way, but there is a huge price to pay for our negligence. After some time, you develop a condition called acidity!

Look around. It is one of the most prevalent complaints that people have. It will be hard to find a person who does not suffer from acidity at one stage of life or another. In fact, it is so common that people don't even go to the doctor to get rid of it. Medicines are available aplenty over the counter with the neighbourhood chemist and everybody helps himself. Chemists must be selling Gelusil, Pudeen Hara, Eno Fruit Salt, Milk of Magnesia and God knows what else, worth crores of rupees every year!

The drugs do reduce the symptoms, but do not solve the problem. The drugs are reducing acidity while you are yourself unintentionally increasing it. You see, taking a medicine is like applying the brakes to a runaway car. Before applying the brakes, you have to ensure that you have lifted your foot off the accelerator pedal. That is what we do while driving. But when it comes to eating, we press the accelerator (eating quickly) while we apply the brakes at the same time (taking a medicine).

Acidity is not the only problem that we have to suffer. Even with the help of excessive acid, the un-chewed food cannot be processed fast enough. As a result, it sits there in the stomach for far too long and starts rotting. So, you are saddled with another problem: gas formation.

Take a simple analogy. When you cook food, some garbage is bound to be generated. You have to dispose it. So, you throw it out either yourself or a maid takes it out for you. Suppose this garbage cannot be sent out

for four-five days, what happens? It starts rotting and stinking. Something quite similar happens inside the stomach, resulting in excessive burping and even bad breath. But, you can take insurance against the gas problem by spending sufficient time with your food.

Incidentally, if you already suffer from a gas problem, please take a few other precautions as well. One, avoid taking beans, especially *urad dal* (black gram). These worsen the condition.

Two, do not take aerated water. Ironically, it is very common to see people take a glass of soda whenever they are suffering from gas. They want to get rid of gas but here they are taking soda water, which is loaded with gas! The end result is that they have a further overload. Due to the excessive amount, they start burping and think that soda is helping them get rid of gas. Nothing could be farther from truth!

Three, you should avoid talking while eating. If you speak while eating, you would swallow a lot of air with the food and it gets trapped inside, aggravating the gas problem. Old-timers will recall that elders used to tell them that it was taboo to speak while eating. Perhaps the reason was scientific rather than religious.

In fact, chewing properly itself helps in solving the gas problem, because when the food is converted into liquid right there in the mouth, the chances of gas getting trapped in the stomach are greatly reduced.

We are so ignorant about the ill effects of gulping food, that at times we see mothers rush out of their houses to the waiting school buses, all the time fervently stuffing food into the mouths of their wards. They are anxious that if their child is not fed sufficiently, he will fall short of nutrients. How wrong they are! Quite the contrary is actually happening.

If the child had not eaten his breakfast, he would have only missed his fats, minerals, vitamins, proteins and so on. But by eating food without chewing it, he is not only being deprived of them but is also saddled with undigested food, which will only add to his weight and misery! Not only that, he is learning to eat too quickly. The same also happens to the adults.

From this week, apply the rule of chewing 32 times to liquids like juices, milk, tea and coffee also. (Only water does not require saliva and can be gulped down quickly.) Take a sip of every liquid without counting but take the next sip ONLY after you have completed the count of 32. That way, even while drinking something you will be producing saliva aplenty. After all, you have to increase the supply from one-fourth of a litre to full three litres!

A practical suggestion to those who are religious minded. Why waste time counting numbers every time you take a morsel? Please notice that counting from one to 32 requires about 20 seconds. Why not recite some *mantra* or *shloka* or *chaupai* during this period? For instance, the widely loved Gayatri Mantra can be recited thrice in 20 seconds. So, don't take the next bite/sip till you have recited the Gayatri Mantra three times.

All this while, have the thought in your mind that, "O Lord Almighty, it is only through your grace that I am alive today," and "I have my daily bread while millions of less fortunate persons go hungry." With this attitude of gratitude, the mundane act of eating the food can be converted into full-fledged meditation.

If you have no time or interest in religion, you can pick up a poem or a song which takes 20 seconds to recite. Make a promise to yourself that you will take the next bite only after you have finished reciting it.

You can devise your own techniques for slowing down. I once met a person who ate far slower than me. I complimented him on his sagacity, but he told me that he had acquired this habit while in school for a very down-to-earth reason. His parents used to be opposed to his watching television and he was allowed to do so only while having meals. He perfected the art of eating so slowly that he could watch the whole serial while doing so. *Touche!*

You will be amazed that by eating this way, your food intake will get greatly reduced. If earlier your hunger was satiated after eating, say four *chapattis* (Indian bread), now you will feel full after just three or even two. The reason for this is very simple.

Your system does not need food but energy. So far, its energy needs were not being fulfilled because the food was in semi-solid form, which it could not handle. Now that you give it duly masticated food, which it can easily digest, it will get the needed energy from far less food.

Take a simple analogy. Suppose, you have run out of cooking oil at home and ask someone to fetch it from the market. This worthy person, instead of bringing the oil or ghee, brings home groundnuts or sunflower seeds. Will these help you in frying something? No doubt, there is oil in groundnuts or sunflower seeds. But you cannot extract it. Similarly, so far you were eating in excess only because your system was saying, "I don't know what you have sent me, but this is not what I can convert." That is why you ended up overeating. The fault was not yours but of the way you had been taught to eat food.

Since many mothers do not know the importance of proper chewing, they end up rushing their children into eating quickly and thus spoiling their health from a very early age.

Are you also one of those millions who just cannot resist a tasty bite, although they later also bemoan their weakness? Please don't blame yourself because you were not at fault. It was only your system's way of force-feeding you when it did not get energy because you were not chewing properly. You couldn't eat too much of ordinary food. So, it made you cross the limits by luring you, through your favourite dishes. Once you start chewing well, you will be amazed that you are able to resist succulent temptations much, much better.

That will do a lot of good to your self-confidence as well. So, it is a win-win situation.

You will find that merely by chewing well, you will start feeling so much lighter. I won't be surprised if you also start losing some weight in the process. Many other advantages are in store. The exercise you give to your jaw will improve the health of your gums and teeth, because adequate chewing cleanses and strengthens them naturally.

The exercise will do a lot of good to your facial muscles. Not only that, the bouts of cough and cold that you occasionally have, will become less frequent. Amazing? Just go ahead and try it. The proof of the pudding lies in the eating, as you know. How does it happen? You will learn, by and by. Right now, follow what the Nike ad says, "Just do it!"

But new good habits take some time to acquire. Like an infant learning to stand, you will slip many a time. In fact, initially you may forget to chew well after just taking one or two bites the right way. Don't feel discouraged. You will remember, by and by, and soon it will become your second nature. Till that happens, I don't mind if you chew only one bite properly during one meal. You will start loving this intensive mastication so much that soon enough, even if you are forced to eat fast, you won't be able to do it.

Happy chewing! Happy living!

Week 4

By now, you must have got quite used to eating slowly, masticating and enjoying every morsel. Our next goal is to know exactly how much to eat, just as we know how much we can run, how many flights of stairs we can climb without turning our legs into jelly and how much weight we can carry (that big suitcase? No way!). Now is the time to know precisely HOW MUCH we can eat; anything more than that would become a burden and a nuisance.

Rather, it is a question of finding out by self-observation, how much we can DIGEST. Stuffing food into the mouth is the easiest thing to do. If you feel like it, you can eat the whole bowl full of *gulab-jamuns* (balls of sweets in sugar syrup) or a whole cake. My word! Many people have actually done that. But the question is: can we digest it?

Ironically, in North India, where I come from, eating in excess is considered a sign of good health. You will find any number of people chiding you for eating "too little." They will taunt you with remarks like: "When I was your age, I could polish off a dozen *paranthas* (Indian fried bread) or omelettes or *rasgullas* (cottage-cheese balls in sugar syrup)." If they also happen to be into drinking, they will tell you how they could gulp down one, two or three bottles every day. In Punjab, even mixing water with alcohol is considered a sissy act. The real macho ones want to drink neat. What a neat way to waste a good life!

It is difficult to explain to them that eating or drinking too much is not a sign of good health but of poor judgement. It is akin to someone saying that my car is so good that it can finish one litre of petrol in covering two kilometres. Using up too much fuel is no bravery, friends. How much you can work with how little food is the actual sign of *fuel efficiency.*

The first thing you must understand is, that eating to your full capacity is not a wise thing to do at all. It is the rough equivalent of driving your car at full speed: there can be a horrifying accident at any time. While we rarely drive our cars at 200 km per hour, we press the eating pedal to the floor almost every week. It hurts for a while and then everything seems to become *normal.* No, it does not. You may forget what you ate; your system does not. It does not forgive either. It hits back with a vengeance – when you are most vulnerable.

You should be familiar with a peculiarity of your digestive system. Like every other part of your body, it takes permission from the brain when to begin eating and when to stop. While all other body parts manage to get such permission in less than one second, the stomach has to wait for full 20 minutes. The consequences are funny – but only when they are being suffered by someone else.

While you are eating, you are certain that you need another *chapatti* or slice of bread or whatever. But after you have washed your hands and had that mandatory round of *saunf* (fennel) or *paan* (betel leaf) or any other mouth freshener, you feel bloated and exclaim: "Oh my God, I have overeaten yet again!" It wasn't your fault that the *Halt* message reached your belly too late, but you would have had to suffer nevertheless. You are not only fully loaded but also overloaded.

There is more to follow. Once gastric juices and the saliva from the mouth are mixed with your food, it expands. The best parallel is the rising of the cake when it is done. Every baker knows that the cake becomes bigger after it is put in the oven. That is how it gets its sponginess. To make sure that it does not spill out of the container, they never fill the batter to the brim. Instead, they keep the container half empty. But what

have we done to our abdomen? Leave alone keeping it half empty; we have already filled it to the brim. When the food rises, it causes everything from unease to disease.

So, the first safety measure you must take is to never eat to your full capacity. As said earlier, that is the rough equivalent of driving at a breakneck speed.

By the way, did you notice that most of us don't overeat at home but over-indulge ourselves when we are on a vacation or have gone to a party? That is actually the worst time to do so. Why? Because in such circumstances, you are most likely not doing any exercise worth the name; you may also be short on sleep and you may also be stressed out.

Actually, you should always make sure – whether you are at home or eating out – that you do not over-indulge yourself. Once you start listening to your body, you will notice that when you have had nearly 60 or 70 per cent of your meal, a tiny voice in your head will tell you to stop. At least it will pose you a question: "Should I eat or should I stop right now?" The moment you face this dilemma, be sure that it is time to STOP.

We all get this warning signal but it is invariably ignored. Even if we know that we should stop, our veto goes in favour of continuing to eat. We have invented many pretexts to justify our eat-on march: it is an insult to the gods to leave food on the plate; it's bad manners; it will be embarrassing that I took too much; now what will happen to the leftovers . . .

If you want to improve your health, let none of these considerations weigh on your mind. The moment you feel you have had enough, leave the rest there and then. No ifs and buts about it. It does not matter whether you throw the leftovers in the bin or you eat it sometime later or you give it to someone else or it is fed to the dogs. You are not to take a morsel more than what you must. It can ruin the fine balance of your digestive system. Let not your belly do the work of a dustbin. If the food has to be thrown into the dump, so be it. It must not be loaded onto your

abdomen. The consequences are too scary to be risked.

And now, to take care of that 20-minute expansion . . . There is a very simple technique to account for that unavoidable eventuality. It will take you the whole of this week to gauge the extent of this expansion. Whenever you complete your breakfast, lunch or dinner, set an alarm for 20 minutes later. For instance, if you are through with breakfast at 8 am, the alarm will be for 8.20 am, and if the lunch is complete by 1.30 pm, the alarm will be for 1.50 pm. These days every mobile phone worth its name has the alarm facility. So you can do this exercise anywhere. The only precaution that you may need to take is to put the alarm on the vibratory mode so that nobody else becomes aware of it.

When the alarm rings 20 minutes after finishing a meal, stop whatever you are doing for a moment and ask yourself an honest question: "Am I feeling bloated, overfed or uneasy?" If you do, it means you ate more than what you could have digested. Now when you eat your next meal, cut down your intake by one or two morsels and check yourself again.

Mind you, you are not to make any drastic reduction in the intake, because that will leave you feeling deprived. Just cutting the intake by a morsel or two will be enough.

Do the same thing during the next meal too. Are you still uncomfortable? Reduce by another morsel. Think of your belly as a car. It can accommodate only five people. Push in more and it will not only slow down but also break down, sooner or later.

Or, learn from a boat. It is safe only as long it carries weight below its maximum capacity. If you cross the limit, it can capsize so very easily. The same is the case with eating. Even one morsel can at times make the difference between *just right* and *too much*.

After eating carefully and consciously for three to four days, you will get to know how much is burdensome for your system and how much is right.

But you have not hit upon the optimum quantity as yet. That will take another few days. Keep on setting the alarm and asking yourself the vital question, but with a twist. Of course, you are no longer feeling uncomfortable 20 minutes after the meal. Now ask yourself: "Am I feeling sleepy?" If you are, your intake is still a little more than what it should be. Let me explain the mechanics of it.

Every cell of the body runs on the energy that you get from the food that you eat. Even your digestive system operates on this energy. To make sure that it is always in working order, some portion of the energy is earmarked for it. So, if say 100 units of energy are produced from the food, about 20 units are kept reserved for the digestive system to take care of the next meal. It is something like a specially dedicated line providing electricity to a powerhouse. Whichever area may suffer a power shutdown, the supply to the powerhouse is provided on priority, because only then can it supply electricity to others.

If we eat more than what we should, the 20 units of energy earmarked for the digestive system will not be enough to take care of the extra bulk. So the supply meant for other parts of the body will have to be diverted to the stomach. This shortfall is made up by reducing the supply to your brain and hence you feel lethargic a few minutes after a meal.

Mind you, this lethargy is different from what you feel because of lack of sleep. If you had a late night, you will feel sleepy the whole day. But the yawns that you get 20 minutes after the meal are because of the excessive food that your digestive system is being made to handle.

Ironically, most people think that just because they are having a good night's sleep means that they are in good health. Nothing could be farther from the truth. A friend of mine used to say that he feels so sleepy after lunch that he wishes to have a dining chair, which after the meal, can be converted into a cosy bed at the press of a button. Excessive sleep is not at all good. We will deal with the subject of sleep in some detail later, but for the time being, please remember the simple rule of the thumb:

Six hours of sleep are a must for an adult, seven hours are a luxury, eight hours is a crime and anything more than that is a sign that you are spoiling your health.

So, if you do feel sleepy after meals, reduce your intake a wee bit. In a week or so, you will know how much food your digestive system processes without straining itself. It will be thankful to you for not shoving in anything more! That is why the conventional wisdom is:

Bhojan adha pet kar, dugna paani peeye. Tiguna shram, chauguni hansi, varsha sawa sau jeeye.

(Fill half your belly with food and twice as much with water. Do thrice as much exercise and laugh four times as much. This is the recipe for a long life of 125 years!)

Let it be added that this conscious eating is also the key to putting brakes on your runaway weight increase. You must remember that the weight does not increase out of the blue. It simply piles up because your input is more than your output. If you eat more than what you should, you are bound to pad up – and at all the wrong places. So, tuck in only what you can comfortably process.

While doing all this, please also be wary of the clever marketing ploy of super sizing. Today, they are selling everything in XXL packages. Instead of 300 ml bottles, cold drinks come in a litre and even one and a half litre bottles. The same holds true of popcorns sold at the malls, which come in buckets large enough to feed five people. But sharing a pack is considered infra-dig.

That does not mean that just because you have bought a popcorn pack all by yourself, you have to eat it all. Learn to eat only as much as you easily can and reject what you can't. Don't even keep it near you after having your fill, because you will tend to eat some more. Out of sight is out of mind.

At home, make it a habit to take food in smaller bowls. Believe it or not, you will be satiated after eating far less. A full but smaller bowl seems more filling to our brain, than a half-full huge bowl.

Happy living!

Week 5

By now, you must be realising that we should eat to live, not live to eat, because if we use the second option, we don't live too long and whatever time we get is not going to be very pleasant. If we eat right we live right. Food not only affects our body but also our mind and heart. That is why it is said: *Jaisa ann, vaisa tann, vaisa mann.* (As you eat, so is your body and so is your mind.)

This fact is acknowledged even by western science: *A healthy mind in a healthy body.*

That means that if you want a healthy mind, you have to have a healthy body. And how do you have a healthy body? By eating rightly, of course. As we have already discussed, you can't eat wrong and yet be disease-free. Howsoever expensive a car may be, it requires the right fuel to run it. So does our amazing body.

So far, we have focussed on *how to eat* and *how much to eat*. We now come down to *what to eat* because WE ARE WHAT WE EAT. We can either eat what is good for us or fill ourselves up with things which eat us up. The choice is entirely ours.

At times, we tend to be as innocent as fish. They see the bait and rush to it, totally ignoring the hook hidden behind it. The most surprising thing is that they don't learn a lesson even when they see one of them getting killed this way. Sure enough; another fish takes the bait!

We are similarly enamoured by taste. We enjoy a succulent food item so much that we ignore what it does to our system. In fact, we are almost ignorant about the functioning of the system till it starts giving us trouble. By then it is too late.

We must wake up to reality about our lifestyle well in time so that we don't pay for our mistakes with our life. Generally, we make three types of mistakes:

1. We eat things that we must avoid
2. We eat too much of them
3. We eat them too quickly

Normally, all three mistakes are made in the case of items that are our favourites. The end result is that food, which is the elixir of life, ends up being its destroyer. What should be borne in mind is that there are only two destinations for the food that we eat. Almost all of it should get converted into energy; and the remainder must be expelled out of the body as waste material quickly. Anything that is left inside becomes the cause of so many maladies (unease, disease, obesity, lack of energy, tension, premature ageing, premature death and so on). Just as it is necessary to eat food, it is also necessary to see that the energy is utilised and the waste material is efficiently disposed off. We fall behind on both counts.

By now you must have realised that by eating too quickly, we are not able to convert food into energy as much as we must. To make things worse, we are also not able to expel the garbage. That is why it is said in our scriptures:

Sarvanam roganam mool karanah kupitah malah.
(The root cause of all diseases is the garbage rotting inside our bodies.)

Just as you have to familiarise yourself with at least the steering wheel, the clutch, the brakes and the accelerator if you have to learn driving, you must know the basics of digestive system if you have to make it run smoothly. In fact, its smooth functioning is essential for the proper running of every other part of the body as well. Let's go over its operation in a simple – rather over-simplified – manner.

Look at the diagram given carefully and then let's discuss it:

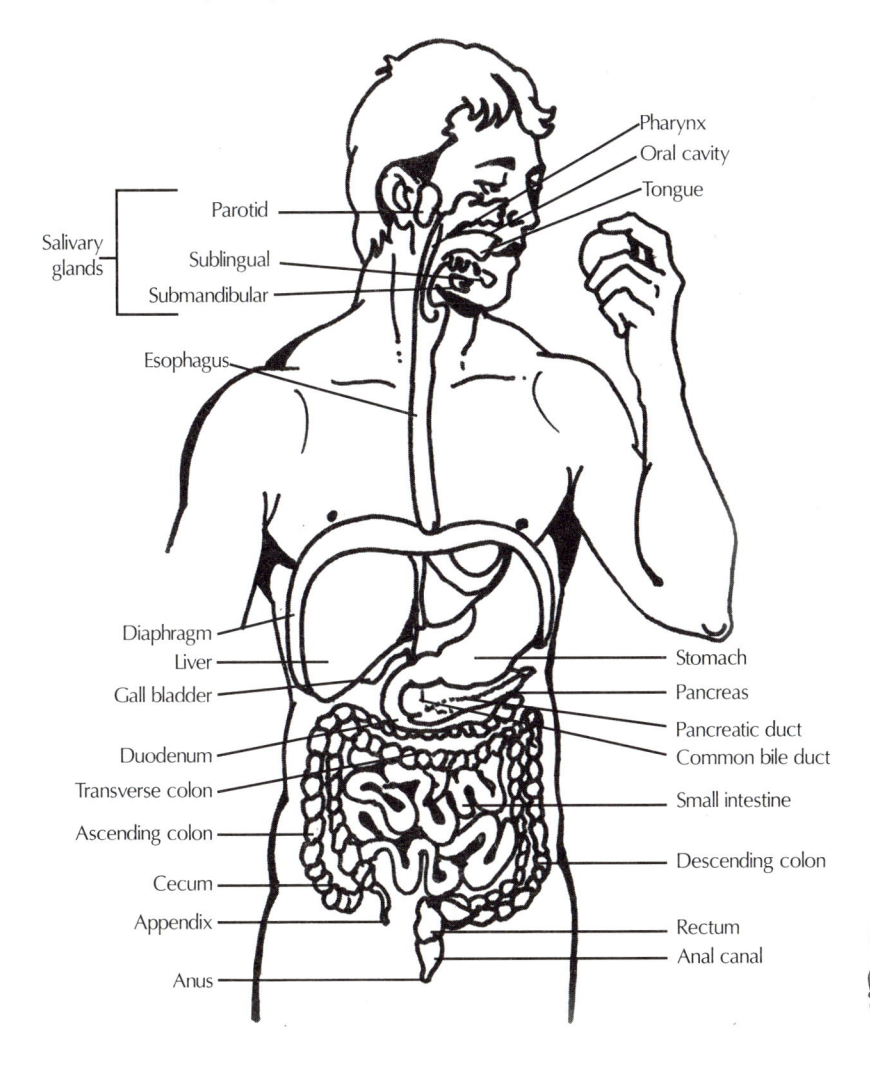

The food that we put in our mouth gets mixed with the saliva – provided we masticate it long enough – and it is then pushed down the gullet. It travels through the oesophagus and enters our stomach. Here all the gastric juices are mixed with it and it is ready for conversion into energy.

It is then pushed into the small intestine through the pyloric valve and some more juices from the liver (gall bladder) and the pancreas are mixed into it to facilitate the amazing transformation of food into energy.

The food is pushed further through a wave-like motion called peristalsis. As the food – which is now called the *chyme* – moves forward, it comes in contact with millions of villi (hair-like protrusions), which play a dual role. They convert food into energy and transport the energy out of the digestive tract into the bloodstream.

By the time the food reaches the end of the small intestine, it is almost waste material. With so much gastric juices mixed with it, it is entirely in liquid form. The wonderful machine called the human body does not waste any of these precious fluids. So, most of the reusable items are re-absorbed in the body during the journey through the large intestine, so that, by the time the waste material reaches the rectum, it is in semi-solid form.

Broadly speaking, the digestive system can be divided into three parts. The mouth and the stomach comprise the storage-cum-mixing plant, the small intestine is the main biochemical factory, while the large intestine is the recycling plant. All these three work in tandem.

These have been allotted specified time in which to finish their work. The stomach is supposed to despatch whatever it has received in four hours; the small intestine completes the digestive job in another four hours, while the large intestine reabsorbs the invaluable chemicals for later use in about eight hours. That makes it a total of 16 hours. The digestive system is also given a grace period of another eight hours, making it a total of 24 hours.

That means that within 24 hours, whatever you have eaten or drunk should either get converted into energy or must go out of the system as waste material.

The speed at which a particular food item moves within the alimentary canal varies greatly. Some items take less than 24 hours, and are called light foods. Some take about 24 hours and are considered standard foods while those that take more than 24 hours are considered heavy foods. In Hindi language, they are called Sattvic, Rajasik and Tamasik foods respectively.

As must be obvious to you, we have to take more of Sattvic and Rajasik foods and very little of Tamasik foods if we have to maintain good physical, emotional and mental health. Unfortunately, most of us do exactly the opposite.

Incidentally, Tamas is connected with night, and devilish forces. Those preferring such items tend to have not only poor heath but also an unsettled nature.

The trouble is, that there are far too many items that come in the Tamasik category and it is a very difficult proposition to eliminate all of them. But we must at least cut out those that take way beyond 24 hours and clog the system for months and years altogether. We will discuss these items from next week onwards. Meanwhile, you prepare yourself for shunning them like a live grenade!

Let me remind you that it is not as if the whole of these items stay in your system for long. They leave behind only a small amount of residue inside and it keeps on accumulating there, causing you all sorts of problems. That is what is called toxic overload.

Understand it this way. When you complain in a hotel that their cutlery is unclean, it does not mean that it is covered with muck. There may be only a fingerprint or a trace of fat sticking to a side of the glass. But that is enough to brand the glass as dirty. In the same way, a bit of residue left inside is enough to be troublesome. Just as we clean all utensils everyday, our inside also has to be squeaking clean every morning. But that hardly ever happens.

This residue, which the digestive system is unable to expel, remains stuck there for too long, causing all types of agony. Have you ever had some food particle stuck inside the gap between two teeth? Remember how irritating the experience is? Your tongue keeps finding the trouble-spot, while you feel terribly uncomfortable. The agony ends only when you find a toothpick. Well, there are toothpicks for taking care of food particles caught inside the mouth. But, how about for the food particles stuck to your entrails? Unfortunately, there are none and you have to suffer unnecessarily. The time has come to eliminate those items that leave behind such obstinate residue.

The beauty of the human digestive system is that if you avoid mistakes for as little as six months, it heals itself and reverses 90 per cent of the damage that has taken place over several decades. The only condition is that during this self-healing process, we must maintain strict discipline and avoid every dangerous item religiously. To accomplish that, join our fraternity, which treats the human body as a holy temple to be respected and to be kept free of all harmful influences.

Have you ever seen horse-carts driven by inhuman cart drivers? There are many of that kind on Indian roads. Suppose the horse has the capacity to carry 10 quintals of weight on the cart, they would overload it to 11 quintals. The horse would be struggling but would be kept burdened, nevertheless.

Some don't stop even at that. They will put 12, 13 or 14 quintals on the cart. The end result is that one day, the horse will either collapse or the cartload may become so heavy that it might lift the horse into the air.

If that happens, it won't be enough to simply reduce the weight to 10 quintals and get the horse going again. You will need to totally unshackle it, let it rest for a few days and only then hitch the cart to it. That is the big price one has to pay for a few days of avarice.

We should realise that our body has been similarly overloaded – and for decades. For a few months, we will have to give it total rest so that it can recoup. A *little bite does not matter and its ok to indulge once in a while*, are alright, but only in the case of a person who happens to have no disease at all and no extra weight as well. But those groaning under the dietary sins of the past have to be very strict if they want to rejuvenate themselves. It is like suffering a fracture. No matter how much weight you were able to carry before you met with the fracture, you have to avoid even one kilogram while your hand is in plaster. So for the time being, consider that your digestive system has suffered a *fracture*. So, you have to postpone your binges for a better tomorrow.

Some want instantaneous results, like two-minute noodles. Six months seems like an eternity to them. When we are trying to wipe out lifestyle sins of decades, six months is nothing. Suppose someone was put behind bars for a decade for a serious crime. He cannot say after one month that he has repented and would never repeat the crime and should be allowed to go home. Good conduct may see him out of the jail, after, say six or seven years, but one or two months are just not enough for regaining freedom. In dietary matters, we should think ourselves lucky that the damage done over decades can be rectified in just six months. A man-made machine might never have gone back on rails at all!

***

Let's now move to the second topic of the week. If you happen to have a mobile phone – who doesn't have one these days – you know well that it has to be charged on a regular basis. And in case you are a heavy user, then your cell phone may be spending one hour to 90 minutes every day hooked on to the charger.

Our body too requires regular *charging* through intensive physical activity or exercise. The only difference is that while the battery of the cell phone runs out in only a few days if not charged, our body can continue to function a whole lifetime without *charging*, although at a greatly depleted levels of energy and with the span of life greatly reduced.

The human body is a dynamic machine which abhors inactivity, so much so that even when an infant is in the cradle, it keeps on moving its hands and legs constantly. As we grow older, we tend to forget this mandatory requirement, with the result that by the time we are middle-aged, we turn into couch potatoes. The result? We function at only 10% of our optimum capacity. Put it this way: instead of giving an output of 100 units per hour, our body gives out only 10 units.

This is being penny wise and pound foolish. Let's calculate the loss that we suffer. Without exercising, our output is 240 units in 24 hours (24 x 10). If only we had set aside 90 minutes for exercise, we would have *worked* for only 22 and a half hours but would have given out 100 units per hour, adding up to a total of 2250 units. Look at the huge difference! It is, as if instead of earning Rs. 240 per day, we would have made Rs. 2250 per day. On a monthly basis, it will be Rs. 7,200 in the first case and Rs. 67,500 in the second. Do you think it's worth it? Then read on.

Yet, the majority suffer this huge loss for three reasons. One, we think we don't have time. Two, exercise is *painful*. And, three, it is quite boring. Let's go over these *reasons* usually bandied about, one by one, and you will realise that they are actually lame excuses.

If by some magic, you could devote the time saved by not exercising to a more *productive* purpose, then I would have been more than happy to go along with the reasoning. Unfortunately, the time you save by being sedentary is spent in being either ill or drained out. You may not have time for exercise, but diseases have all the time in the world to keep you company. Have you ever met a man who could escape illness just because he was too busy to be on a sickbed? On the contrary, those who ignore their body not only remain sickly all their life, but also reach the end of the rope sooner than they should.

Yet, we take that risk, day in and day out. In younger days, most of us do have an exercise regime. But it is conveniently forgotten when we are past our prime. Actually, that is the time when you need to be limbering up the most. In youth, you were fairly active throughout the day and even if you did not set aside any time for exercise, it did not matter. However, now that you are glued to the chair for several hours due to the *cushy* job that you have landed, there is no choice but to compensate for the inactivity by devoting 90 minutes or so to an invigorating exercise regime.

The same is true of pain also. Yes, if you exercise there will be pain but it will go away after some time. But the pain that you will get by remaining stationary will not leave you for a long, long time. Ask someone who has had heart trouble, what it feels like?

Most people find exercising boring because of its repetitive nature. Really? Then how can you eat repeatedly? That, too, is equally monotonous. If you do one, then you just have to do the other too. In fact, if you are a food lover, you have no chance of avoiding exercise.

To begin with, you don't have to devote a full 90 minutes. You can start with as little as 15. All that is needed is regularity and a commitment to do so, seven days a week. Ok, ok, you can take a weekly off, but don't do less than six days a week, although I would prefer that you work *overtime* to compensate for the leisurely rest you might have had for the past few years.

Once your body knows that you are regular like a clock, it will start responding in a magnificent way. It is a strange contraption indeed. The more rest you give it, the more it will ache and pain. The more you work out, the better you will feel, because exercise stimulates feel-good chemicals like endorphin and serotonin.

There are various forms of exercise, but for a beginner, there is nothing better and simpler than walking. Start with this elementary *charging* of the body and then gradually you can graduate to more strenuous exercises.

What is important is establishing a habit. The very act of getting ready and going out will provide many benefits. Unfortunately, most people go for a walk only as a hobby, to be done on days when they have nothing better to do. But those 35 to 45 minutes of power walking should be your top priority, come hail or shine.

A few basic precautions are in order. First, always wear sports shoes while going out for a walk. It is not uncommon to see people walking in parks in formal shoes or even, bathroom slippers. That is sure to leave you with aching feet, and ultimately you may give up walking. Sports shoes, on the other hand, encourage you to walk more. In fact, it will be a good idea to wear them even when you go out to the market and so on.

Second, prefer to walk outdoors instead of working out on a treadmill. Fresh, outside air has a magical effect on our health. Early morning is, of course, the best time to do so. But if you cannot do so in the morning, please don't give it a total go-by. Any time is walking time. I have seen people in tuxedos in London coming down from their swanky offices near the Thames, taking out sneakers from the boots of their cars and doing several rounds of the parks nearby. Just do it, whatever the time is. You can use the treadmill on days when it is not possible to go out because of rain or snow.

Week 6

Last week, we talked about how certain food items clog your system for a very long time. Now the time has come to banish them from your diet. If you can do so forever, it will be a great service to your body. But even if you decide to do so for just six months, you will be able to regain much of your health. Once you are back to normal, it will not harm you all that much even if you commit some dietary excesses, once in a while.

One of the biggest enemies of health is *maida*, or refined flour. In a way, I would count it as a bigger enemy than even alcohol, because at least when you drink, you are aware of the consequences. But we eat refined flour indiscriminately, day in and day out. So, it ends up doing much more harm. Since almost everyone eats it, the total damage it causes is nothing less than catastrophic.

It clings to the entrails, virtually like cement, and it is next to impossible to get rid of. Because of its longer-than-usual stay in the digestive system, it rots and causes all sorts of complications.

Most people prefer it to simple whole-wheat *atta* (flour) for two reasons. One, the items made out of *maida* are whiter in colour, and two, they have a smoother texture. What they forget is that the looks are deceptive and hide a dangerous property that gives you everything from indigestion to constipation (due to removal of bran or roughage) to malnutrition to even diabetes and cancer. It is also a contributing factor in ischemic heart disease, diverticular disease, hiatus hernia, gallstones, polyps of the colon, cancer of colon and rectum, varicose veins, obesity and haemorrhoids.

What needs to be underlined is that we have no objection to *atta* as such. Some people in their ignorance keep off carbohydrates strictly. There is no need to do so. The real villain is the *maida* that has the tendency to clog the system. Whole-wheat flour has enough fibre to ensure that it is slowly and effectively digested. Refined flour, on the other hand, has characteristics quite opposed to that of *atta* and feeds numerous diseases. The removal of the outer husk transforms it into a dangerous substance, but we eat it in abundance due to its taste.

As you know water (H_2O) is made up of hydrogen and oxygen. When these two are together in a water molecule, they retard fire. But hydrogen and oxygen atoms separately aid fire. In the same way, *atta* from wheat is *Mr Good* while *maida* is *Mr Bad*.

So, what are the items made out of *maida*? Here is a small list to get you started. I am sure you can add many more popular items to the list:

1. Naan 2. Bhatura 3. Papri/Golgappe 4. Matthi 5. Noodles 6. Pasta (Macaroni, etc) 7. Bread 8. Cake 9. Pastry 10. Biscuits 11. Gulabjamun 12. Burgers 13. Sewian 14. Samosa 15. Patties 16. Spring Rolls 17. Puri 18. Bread pakora 19. Balushahi 20. Parantha 21. Pizza 22. Hot Dog 23. Kulcha 24. Gujia 25. Ghevar 26. Jalebi 27. Momos 28. Swiss Roll

As you can see, it is a staple of most sweets and savouries and is used extensively in bakery. The time has come to say it a firm goodbye, at least, till you have sufficiently recovered your health.

Wherever possible, replace *maida* with *atta*. As you must have noticed, after spoiling the health of the people for many decades, makers of noodles have now started shifting to whole-wheat noodles. We have to force them to do that with each and every item. But then there are some foods which just cannot be made out of *atta*. In their case, just banish them from your menu for the time being. Your system will be thankful to you for this small mercy.

A word of caution here – some people think that brown bread is made out of *atta*. This many not be true in all cases. Some unscrupulous bakers have been only adding brown colour to the bread made out of *maida* as a propaganda ploy. You have to go in for actual whole-wheat bread.

Maida also rules because items made from it have a longer shelf life. But you should focus more on your own life than on the life of the food items. Even if you think that such items are part of your lifestyle, please remember that you will be able to follow a lifestyle only if you have life. Take my word. *Maida* is one of the most ruthless public enemies, and the sooner you push it out of your house, the better.

Noted nutritionist Carl C. Pfeiffer, Ph. D., M. D. says in *Mental And Elemental Nutrients*: "During World War II Denmark stopped refining flour, an action which was not accompanied by any other marked changes in living habits. Later it was found that the death rate had dropped and that there had been a marked decline in cancer, heart disease, diabetes, kidney trouble, and high blood pressure."

Another authority, Rex Newnham, laments: "Laboratory animals cannot live for more than a few weeks on white bread, yet most of us like eating this denatured and impoverished food."

Vitamin A, vitamin E, vitamin C, niacin, riboflavin, thiamine, inositol, folic acid, folinic acid, biotin, vitamin B6, vitamin B12, choline, para-amino benzoic acid, pantothenic acid, alpha-lipoic acid, calcium, phosphorous, magnesium, sodium, potassium, iron, copper, manganese, cobalt, molybdenum, and zinc are lost during the refining process and what we eat is empty food which has been robbed of most of its nutrients. According to one estimate, *maida* has 83 per cent less nutrients than *atta*.

It is really unfortunate that the part that is the best for the humans in the wheat grain is discarded for the use of animals, and what is most harmful is saved up for the use of the *modern* man.

Another major problem attached with refined flour is that it is extremely easy to overeat. The high bulky fibre of whole grain flour satisfies hunger with fewer calories while *maida* items encourage hunger and gorging. Eating it in even small quantities can be dangerous. Consuming it in excess is a sure fire recipe for disaster.

It is also the easiest way to become obese. That is why it is so difficult to find fat people in primitive cultures while they are omnipresent in the so-called modern societies.

By shifting to rich, unrefined complex carbohydrates, you will start your wonderful journey to an enviable body full of life, vigour and energy. Moreover, you will feel happier and contented.

Let me repeat, again and again, that carbohydrates are not our enemy. In fact, they are our most precious friends. Our body runs on them. Every cell of our body needs them to work properly and efficiently. Our brain also runs on the glucose supplied by carbohydrates. Muscles store carbohydrates as glycogen. Your mood, memory and sleep patterns worsen if you eliminate carbohydrates. So don't think of going on a low- carbohydrate, high-protein diet. That will only lead to weakening of muscles and loss of water weight. It will look good on the weighing scale but will ruin your life. All that you have to cut out is refined flour. Just replace it with good old atta and you will be on track to optimum health.

***

So how has your *walking* been going? Have you got used to the routine of getting up early, getting ready and going out, even if it is only for 15 minutes? I am sure you did it for at least six days last week? Good.

Since you have crossed the threshold of pain and lethargy, now you can change gear. Try to spend a few minutes extra on this wonderful activity. In fact, it is not *spending* but *investing*. Even while you are walking, you are actually doing productive work because it will improve the quality of your work, whether you are in business or a job or are a professional.

Please remember that every day we are supposed to take at least 10,000 steps if we have to keep our body in working order. Everyone thinks that he takes that many steps during his various chores. Actually, one does not take more than 4,000 steps that way. So a walk for 6000 steps is an absolute must. That, depending on your speed, can take 50 to 65 minutes. That means that even if you have begun by walking for only 15 minutes a day, your target should be to increase it to 60 minutes or so.

If you are planning to lose weight also, then be prepared to spend more time. That will be the golden hour, which will give you more benefits than any of the other 23 hours. So, never encroach on this sacred hour. What a pity that whenever we are short of time, we eat quickly, skip exercise and postpone prayers. From now onwards, let others make these mistakes; not you, please.

Once you have become *addicted* to your daily walk, divide the time you are devoting to it into three equal parts. For example, if you walk for 30 minutes, make three segments of 10 minutes each. For the first 10 minutes walk at a gentle, slow pace. This will be the warm-up period. The second part can be as brisk as you can make it. And the third part, which will be for cooling down, should again be at a slow pace. Keep changing gears this way and you will be able to avoid cramps and pains, which come to those who are over-enthusiastic while starting on a walking regime and go full steam ahead.

Moreover, do take care that at least the brisk walk should not be done on a hard surface because that can leave you with aching knees. If you look around carefully, you will surely find grassy, or at least, *kutcha* (non-metalled) tracks in your neighbourhood on which you can walk briskly.

One more suggestion: it will be a good idea to eat something – even if it is only a few raisins before you set out for your morning walk. If you are walking on an empty stomach, you will feel run down after some time.

Some think that they do enough work at home, anyway. Let me remind them that repetitive actions do not really comprise exercise. They tire you, but do not give due benefits. For example, washing clothes for two consecutive hours will only hurt your back, and will not be a substitute for a brisk walk.

Next week, we will set out on a wonderful journey into the yoga world. Till then!

Week 7

It is so very sagacious that you have banished *maida* from your diet. The refined flour was the culprit behind many of the problems you had been having. You will miss it for some days, but once you start regaining your vim and vigour, you will regret why you had patronised it in the past at all.

Breaking off with it finally is a very sensible decision, but it is an item that tends to stay in the system for years, and we cannot afford to wait for that long. We want to get rid of it in a matter of months, if not immediately. The time has come to make special efforts towards that.

Just as you need a thorn to pull out another thorn, we will use the whole-wheat flour to undo the damages caused by refined flour. All that you have to do is to increase the amount of bran or roughage in your flour.

Go to any flourmill and buy some bran, which is called *choker* in Hindi. This is the *waste material* that is removed from whole grain flour and left out for animals (what a pity!). Buy a few kilograms of it and roast it in a dry pan till it becomes golden brown. Now start adding one spoon of it per person to the dry flour whenever you are ready to make dough. You can also premix it in your flour canister but if you do it daily, you can increase or decrease its quantity as per taste.

This item is also sold as wheat bran in fancy packages. If you want to go in for those, it is entirely your choice, but the results are the same.

Another item that you can add occasionally to the flour is Isabgol or *psyllium* husk, which is also the outer covering of a grain. Perhaps you have taken it for constipation. Now you can mix it with flour itself. It is fibre only and does not cause any side effects while making your bowel movement smoother.

Go in for the ordinary variety, which also happens to be the most effective. To make more money some companies have started refining Isabgol also and mixing sugar in it. That makes it costly, but does not add to great quality, except that this variety is easier to eat (raw Isabgol happens to stick to the mouth). But since we are not swallowing it in any case and only mixing it with flour, we don't have to go in for costlier brands.

Also add a teaspoon of flaxseeds per person to your flour and a pinch of salt and see how light the *chapattis* made of this mixture are on your system. In fact, you should conduct an experiment. Eat a morsel of such a chapatti raw, without mixing it with *dal* or *sabzi* (lentil or vegetable curry). You will be surprised that after proper mastication for a few seconds, it will start tasting sweet. That is because it is so easy to digest that it turns into glucose right in your mouth on coming in contact with the saliva, and does not put any burden at all on the digestive system.

Since you have added lightly toasted bran to the flour, *chapattis* will look blackish, plus they will also be harder to chew. There is a simple trick to overcome these stumbling blocks. Start making stuffed *chapattis*, by adding chopped vegetables or boiled potatoes and so on, to the dough. Last night's *dal* or *sabzi* can also be added. That will not only make *chapattis* softer but will also mask their dark colour. And, they are more delicious and nourishing too.

In fact, this is also the time to go in for multi-grain *atta*. To your simple wheat flour, you can start adding the flour of following grains:

1. Gram
2. Soyabean
3. Barley
4. Jowar
5. Bajra

In fact, any coarse grain will be just as fine. Each variety of grains has its own qualities and you can benefit from them all. Mind you, this *atta* is not only good for diabetics, but for everybody.

Multi-grain *chapattis* help in cleaning up the system. You will notice that *chapattis* made out of such coarse grains have to be chewed rather well. So, you will have the advantage of extracting more energy from every morsel. They may not taste as good as your *maida chapattis*, but they are far healthier. So put taste on the second spot, behind your health.

***

It is good that you have become used to the daily walk. Now is the time to focus on increasing the flexibility of your joints. Remember, you are only as young as your joints are supple. The best way to keep them nimble is through yoga. Here, a bit of explanation is necessary.

Whenever one talks of *yoga*, the image that forms in the listeners' minds is that of a semi-clad yogi doing certain complicated exercises (called *asanas*). Most think that this is all there is to yoga. Nothing could be farther from the truth.

While postures are indeed an integral part of yoga, they don't comprise yoga, which encompasses much more. To focus on just one aspect will be like several blindfolded persons touching an elephant at different points and reaching a conclusion as to what it looks like. Someone touching its feet will perceive that an elephant is like a pillar; someone touching his abdomen will think it is like a drum while the person touching its tail will be certain that it looks like a rope. They will not be wrong; but they won't be right either.

So, what's real yoga? In the simplest terms, it is a way of living, which helps you to rise to your full potential and then merge with your higher self. There are eight limbs or stages of it:

1. Yama
2. Niyama
3. Asana
4. Pranayam
5. Pratyahaar
6. Dharana
7. Dhyana
8. Samadhi

Performing only yoga *asanas* would be like trying to raise an eight-storey house of which you have not made the first two storeys. The details of what these various stages can be read in any yoga book. For our purpose here, it is sufficient to say that yoga entails certain do's and don'ts for the practitioner. These relate to:

1. First person (the practitioner himself)
2. Second person (his family members and dependants)
3. Third person (the world in general)

It will be presumptuous on my part to request you to fulfil all three duties, but you should fulfil at least the responsibilities that you have towards your own self. That is where physical yoga comes in.

Here, let's understand it in its simplest form. Our body is a machine, like a car, for instance. Now, to run a car smoothly, you have to keep various parameters in mind: oil, air pressure in tyres, battery condition, gear oil, brake pads, and so on. Similarly, the body can also function properly only when many such do's and don'ts are followed. If not, it starts deteriorating. *The combined list of all these rules, which make the body function at its optimum capacity, is called 'yoga'.*

Human body is more complicated than any man-made machine. It has emotions, intellect and mind. These affect its performance. So in the case of humans; peace and a stress-free environment are also very important. Just as one has to have the right type of cable or wi-fi connection to link a computer to the Internet, the human body has also to connect with the super-conscious to be in harmony and rhythm. *The regimen that links us with our inner self is higher yoga.*

When all aspects are covered in an integral manner, the benefits that accrue border on the miraculous. The most noticeable result is that one is able to get rid of 90 per cent of one's supposedly incurable diseases merely through this regime. Not only that, one is also able to prevent most of the common diseases. There are many other bonus improvements. These are listed below:

- Health shows dramatic improvement
- Excessive body weight is shed
- One looks better
- Energy levels increase
- One is more at peace with oneself and one's friends and relatives
- One is stress-free
- One copes with crises more easily
- One lives longer
- The quality of life is much better
- Tension is a thing of the past
- Mental faculties sharpen
- One can grasp most situations easily
- Inter-personal relationships improve
- Family life improves

To enjoy so many benefits, all one has to do is to practise them religiously. In as little as six months, most ill effects of previous mistakes committed because of lack of awareness are eliminated and a new personality takes birth. One only has to be willing to follow the precepts honestly.

Today, we embark on an exciting programme of simple but effective yoga *asanas*, which anyone from eight to eighty can do without fear of injury.

All our joints need to be limbered up. We will add a few exercises every week so that we can take care of every joint from toes to head in a span of 30 minutes or so. Here are three *asanas* for the coming week:

Exercise No. 1:

We begin with the first joint, which is at the base of our toes. Sit with your legs spread in front of you. Just curl your toes away from you to the last millimetre, so that you can feel the stretch not only in the toes but also in your calves and maybe also thighs. Once the mild pain starts, begin counting from one to 10 and then relax. See how good it feels.

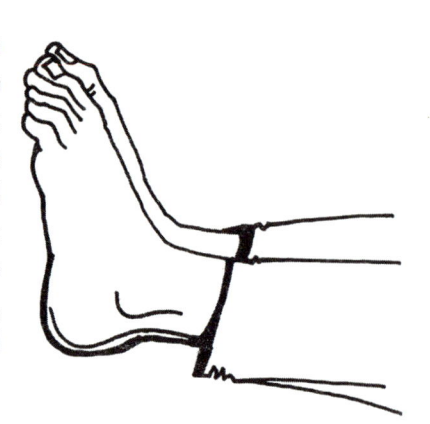

Now is the time to pull the toes towards you. Please remember that you must not only pull to the maximum extent possible but also hold the stretch to a count of 10. This way by alternating, curl the toes away from you and towards you 20 times, holding up to the count of 10 every time. You need not hold your breath at any stage. If you do it right, the pain will be felt not only in your calves but also your thighs.

Exercise No. 2:

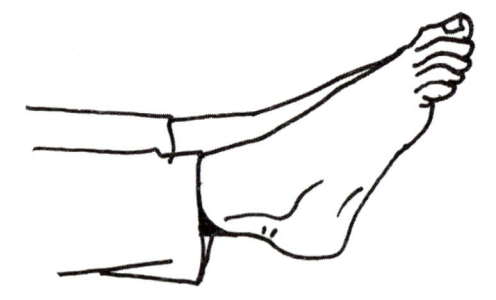

Now use your heels as the fulcrum and push the entire feet away from you. Again hold to the count of 10. Then pull them towards you. Do it 10 times in each direction, 20 repetitions in all.

Exercise No. 3:

This time, push right foot away from you, and the left foot towards you. It will appear as if you are pressing the accelerator, and removing your other foot from the clutch. Hold for the count of 10. Change the feet. Now you will be lifting your right foot from the accelerator and pressing the clutch pedal with the other. This way, do 20 repetitions in all.

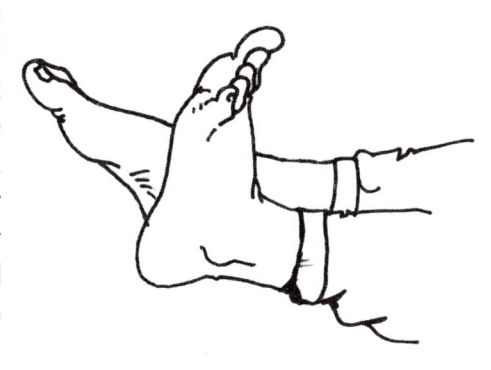

Once you get into the groove, please notice that if these *asanas* are done with your eyes closed and the attention focused on the parts that are being stretched, the simple exercises turn into a meditation. Keep your eyes shut after you have completed the exercise while the attention remains firmly at the toes or the ankle. When you open the eyes after a few seconds, you may find yourself filled with new peace and energy. Try it.

These three exercises will hardly take you five minutes. We will add some more in the weeks to come. The best time to do so will be in the morning. But if you just cannot find time early in the day, then you can do it any time you like. In fact, you can decide never to watch TV while sitting idle. Just unfold your mat and you can do these simple *asanas* while watching the TV.

Make them an integral part of your life. Even such simple exercises can do you tremendous good. Once you have mastered the basics, you can graduate to more advanced exercises.

Week 8

The time has come to vanquish your dietary enemy number two. After you have done so, you will realise how high a price you were paying for your innocent love for tasty bites.

Many centuries ago, nutritionists found that the most wonderful diet for human beings was milk. But there was a small print: they were talking about mother's milk. But this miraculous liquid could be available only for the first one year of one's life or a little longer. So, they decided to look at the animal kingdom so that the benefits could be derived all one's life.

They hunted around, but no milk came anywhere close to mother's milk. They lowered their standards to find out the second best alternative. The desperate search ended at goat's milk. It was the best that could be had from the animal kingdom.

But there were two seemingly small but significant problems. One, it smelled a lot (you could feel the smell even when you burped hours after consuming it). Two, the goats gave so little milk that it was not possible to supply it to millions of people.

So the search was expanded and they decided to settle for the third best. This time it was the cow, which got the place of honour. There was no strong smell to worry about; rather, this milk smelled nice. But the other problem still remained. There were no hybrid cows in those times, and the ordinary ones yielded very little milk.

So, in desperation they decided to take even buffalo's milk. Since the supply was abundant, it soon became the most established source. There were digestion problems galore, but these were all overlooked in the light of larger benefits. It was something like the use of the car. We all know it causes pollution, depletes fossil fuel and adds to noise worries, so on and so forth, but since there is no viable alternative, it is still the favoured mode of transport, regardless.

Over the years, the world has got fairly well used to buffalo milk. But the problem arises when we start concentrating it. So, that glass of thick milk with dollops of *malai* (cream) swimming on top—the painstaking result of a *halwai* (specialised cook of Indian sweets) working for hours over his huge *kadhai* (wok)— tastes divine but can play havoc with your digestive system.

But we are so keen to enhance taste – and, unintentionally, our misery – that we concentrate it even further. Soon enough, it takes the shape of *rabri* (thickened sweet milk pudding). Ah, how fantastic fresh *jalebis* (fried rings of refined flour dipped in sugar syrup) taste when partaken along with rich *rabri*. But your digestive system does not like at all what your taste buds do. It protests in every way it can. Very few listen to it.

Equally dangerous is cream, that integral part of ice-creams and a million other delicacies. They, too, put an untold burden on the system and yet we use them without care.

However, the real atom bomb is our good old *khoya* (thickened solidified milk), which gives us everything from *peda* to *barfi* (Indian sweets). It is as effective as *maida* in ruining your health. Yet, so little is known about it that it is eaten day in and day out. It sticks to your entrails like glue; and due to it, even those food items, which would have otherwise passed through easily, get blocked.

Since we do not know its dangerous characteristics, we add it to our *sabzis*, making sure that it becomes ten times more difficult to digest. In fact, it is added to almost all delicacies, putting your digestive system out of order. Remember one adage about it:

Jisne khaya khoya, usne apna sab kuchh khoya!
(Anyone who eats *khoya* loses everything he has!)

The biggest problem with this man-made poison is that it is very easy to take it in abundance because it is so small and looks so harmless, besides tasting excellent. But these positive qualities hide a killer.

So at least for the next six months, say a total goodbye to *Mr. Khoya*. I can assure you that it will be available later also, and if you think that you have not gained anything by sacrificing *khoya* items, you can always resume eating them.

Cheese, too, can be dicey. So, postpone the intake of that also, particularly while you are in the recovery period. How much you eat matters a lot. Cottage cheese is not quite as hazardous as processed cheese, but you must be careful about portion sizes. Two or three pieces of it are fairly healthy. But when we have it as *matter-paneer* or *shahi paneer*, we tend to go overboard. Exercise caution.

The best way to make it a murderer is by deep-frying it. Unfortunately, that is how some prefer to eat it. It is time you pledged never to do that.

Needless to say, butter and ghee also come into the *alarming* category. You need so little of them, and even that can be skipped if you are over-weight or have any illness. There are comfortable replacements for them, but we will come to them a little later. Right now, just cut down the quantity of butter and ghee drastically.

Talking of milk, please remember that the liquid which is sold today is only broadly similar to what was sold 50 years ago or more. And we are not yet even talking about the practice of making synthetic milk which is nothing less than witches' brew prepared with the help of such poisonous substances as urea and white paint. That is pure poison. Even regular milk that is sold after due checks has undergone a sea change.

Cows and buffaloes were fed grass half a century ago and they had to undergo considerable exercise to reach their green acres. Not any longer. They are fed a rich diet, right there in dairy farms, which is quite similar to the junk food that the humans themselves have. The result is that they yield more milk, which is also thicker, but instead of being more beneficial, it is harder to digest.

Our fetish for *thickness* of milk has done us in. We believe that the thicker it is the better it is. Many a milkman has faced the ire of the buyers, just because his milk was not thick enough. To cater to this irrational demand, an attempt has been made to increase the fat content of milk. The fact of the matter is that creamy milk is a burden on the system. You will be better off going for the skimmed variety. Do not think it is any less useful just because it costs less. Actually, it may be the best for you and your kids.

With this second hidden enemy going out of your system, your road to optimum health will become smoother and you will discover new springs of energy and peace in the days to come. Amen.

***

How is the exercise programme going? Initially, it may be cumbersome, but soon enough, you will fall in love with it. Please remember that the benefits of any good habit that you develop, take some time to flow.

Today, we will add three more ankle exercises to our repertoire:

Exercise No. 4:
Put your feet together in front, with your toes facing skywards, the big

toes together. Now move all the 10 toes towards the left, till the smallest toe of the left foot touches the ground. If necessary, you can put the entire right leg on top of the left one. Count up to 10. Then move all toes towards the right and hold to the slow count of 10. Repeat 10 times on each side, making it a total of 20 repetitions.

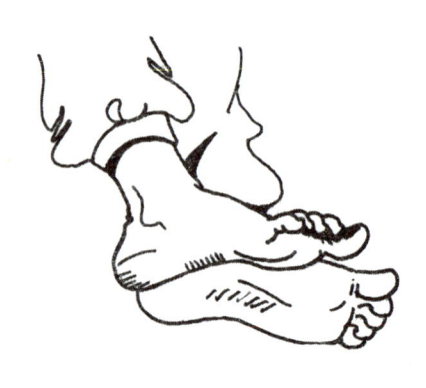

The action will appear as if wipers of a car are moving from left to right, the only difference being that you will be stopping for a count of 10 when you reach the left and right extremity. The stretch of this exercise can be felt right up to your stomach.

This exercise and most of other ankle exercises are done best when you are lying down. So you can also try them out when you have woken up in the morning but are not in the mood to get up. Do them lying down and you will be more energetic on leaving the bed.

Exercise No. 5:
Now keep your feet in front of you at about one foot apart. Turn the toes of both feet inwards, so that they touch the ground in the centre. In other words, the toes of the left foot will turn towards the right and those of the right foot will turn towards the left. Hold to a count of 10.

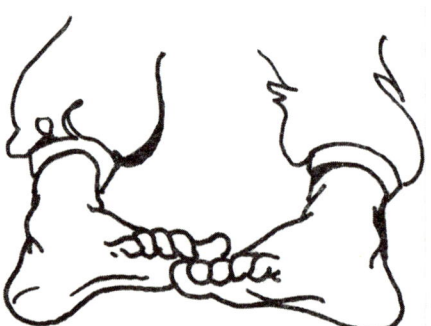

Now move the toes, using the heels as a fulcrum in the opposite direction. The left toes move towards the left till the smallest toe touches the ground while the right toes move towards the right and the smallest touches the ground. Hold to a count of 10.

In this way, turn inwards 10 times and also outwards 10 times, every time holding to a count of 10.

The motion will be akin to the wipers of the Honda Civic moving during the rain. (I do not know why they chose a movement which is the exact opposite of most other cars. Perhaps they wanted to set an example for those who learn this exercise from this book!)

Exercise No. 6:

Again sit with your feet together in front of you; the big toes of the two feet touching, as at the beginning of Exercise No. 4. Imagine that your toes are at the centre of a clock, placed in front. Take the toes to 12, by pushing them farthest from you; hold for a few seconds. Now bring them towards you and you will reach 6. Again hold for some time. This way, take them to 12 and 6 repeatedly 20 times.

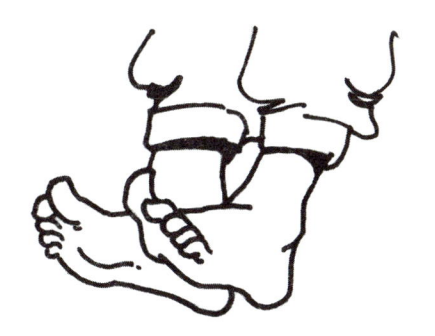

In the same way, 3 will be towards the right and 9 towards the left. Move them from left to right and right to left 10 times, as in Exercise No. 4.

Finally, rotate the toes from 12 to 3, hold, then on to 6 and hold, go to 9 and hold and then go on to 12. That completes one circle. Now complete the next circle in counter clockwise direction. In this way make a total of 20 circles.

Please do not go too fast. And stop for sufficient length of time at 12, 3, 6 and 9. Remember, these are a range of motion exercises and you must try to go to the extreme points in the range.

To show to yourself that half measures don't work, draw the same circles without stretching yourself. They will just not be the same.

That completes the *sukshma asanas* or simple exercises for the ankles. Next week, we will go on to a very important joint—the knee joint. It is either disused or misused, leading to all sorts of problems. We will exercise it in a scientific manner.

Week 9

Let me begin the chapter with a simple question. Suppose you have wheat flour and want to make a *chapatti* or bread or cake out of it. Which is the essential ingredient without which you just cannot do so?

Yes, you guessed it right. It is water. Without water, you just cannot make any of these things.

Now, suppose you are making one *chapatti*. Would one teaspoon of water suffice? Perhaps not. You will need half cup of water or may be even more.

Exactly the same thing happens in our body also. One, we need water. In fact, we need this original no-calories drink with no vitamins, no carbohydrates, no energy, even more than our food. We can survive without food for several days. But water! Try going without it for even a few hours, especially in summers or when you are thirsty.

Two, we need it in sufficient quantity. The human machine is strange. When you are very thirsty, even one sip would seem like a miracle, but it does not fulfil your need. We do drink water but not in sufficient quantity.

Actually, most of us take in water only when we are thirsty. That is like watering your plants AFTER they have dried up. Some of them may survive; some may not. Water is almost free, and yet we have too little of it. Many of our ailments can be attributed to the shortage of water.

You will be amazed if your body could tell you how much it really needs. Here is a rule of thumb for calculating your requirements. What time do you get up in the morning? 7 am, did you say? Fine. And what is your sleep time? May be 11 pm? Ok. That means you are awake 16 hours a day. That is the average, give or take one or two hours.

You need as many glasses of water in a day as you are awake. So, if it is 16 hours, you will need 16; if it is 15 hours then it may be 15 glasses.

Mind you, we are talking of the time when the temperature is average. In very hot months, you may need even more. If you go in for heavy exercise, the need may increase still further.

Many people think that they get sufficient water through tea or coffee that they drink. Nothing could be farther from the truth. If you are a tea/coffee lover, you may have to drink extra water.

Since we are not camels, we cannot take all that water in one go. The sensible way to take it is one glass (about 200 ml) every hour. There is no need to do so at an exact time. Just keep an eye on whether you have taken the elixir for a particular hour. For instance, you should get used to thinking right from 6.45 pm, that you have to take your 7 pm-glass of water. Whether you do so at 6.45 or 7.15, it does not matter. Just do not forget to drink that glass of water.

But, what about the advice given by many doctors that you should take 8-10 glasses per day? My friend, that is the very minimum that you just have to drink. You will be better off if you went above that minimum threshold. But if 15 glasses indeed appears to be excessive to you, you can start with just 8-10 and then build it up. It will be much better than the average people who do not go beyond 3-4 glasses per day.

It will be a good idea to drink water regularly during the day time and then taper down the quantity during the night, because if we continue to do so right up to the bed time, you may have to wake up several times during the night to go to the washroom, thereby disturbing your sleep.

However, please do take at least half a glass of water just before going to bed. It can lead to sound sleep.

Since very little is known about the subject, you may be told scary stories by those who do not take adequate quantities of water themselves. One prevalent myth is that taking *excessive* amounts of water can lead to water retention. The fact of the matter is that water retention happens more to those who are miserly about drinking water and so their bodies start hoarding it.

There are others who think that too much of water may be bad for kidneys and so on. While those already suffering from kidney trouble have to ration their water intake indeed, it is almost impossible for a normal person to have too much of water, because the system can be overloaded only if someone takes upwards of 90 glasses per day. I don't think any sane person will do so!

There are some who say that they just don't like the taste of water. Perhaps that is because it is totally tasteless (at least pure water is). For them, there is a simple solution. One day, boil some green cardamom (*chhotti ilaichi*) in water, filter it and cool it. See if you like the taste. Next day you can also try out boiling aniseeds (*saunf*) and then cinnamon (*dalchini*). You will find drinking at least one of them much easier.

You will find that as your water intake increases, your hunger will also subside. You will feel full after taking far less food. That happens because many of us mistake our thirst to be hunger.

There is a lot of controversy about whether one should take water with food or separately. Actually, the advice to avoid water with meals is meant for those with a yogic lifestyle who take very little food. Others who take a lot of *masala* (spices) and *mirchi* (chilli) need not keep off water.

But it is a very good idea to take a sip or two of warm water after the meals. You will find it easier to digest food and even those with heart complications will find it less troublesome after meals.

Even during the rest of the day, avoid very cold water. The water from an earthen pitcher or a *surahi* is the best option. Refrigerated water is neither good for digestion nor for your throat.

If possible, try to take 3-4 glasses of water on an empty stomach the first thing in the morning. It benefits you in more than one ways. The first advantage is that the shortage of water that may have come about while you were sleeping will be taken care of. After all, you need water even during the night but do not consume it because you are asleep most of the time. Two, water is the most effective and harmless way to induce satisfactory bowel movement.

In fact, take lukewarm water with a little bit of lemon juice and a bit of salt (no honey, please). The trick lies in not going to the toilet for 20 minutes after that and spending this time in a standing position. Ideally, the time should be spent in walking or doing light exercises.

The lemon-water helps in removing food residue sticking to your entrails. Every other laxative has side-effects. This has none.

***

It is exercise time now. This week we are going to take care of a very important joint, which is also the most misused. It is the knee joint. It carries the weight of our entire body and yet we treat it so shabbily. It is time we gave it some tender care.

Before we start exercising it, please remember that even the ankle exercises that we did last week are very helpful in relieving the pressure on the knees. Now we will strengthen the joint itself.

Exercise No. 7:

Standing, bend forward and cover your knees with your palms. Imagine that you are standing atop a clock. The 12 will be in front of you, 3 will be to your right, 6 will be behind you and 9 will be towards your left.

Bend some more so that your knees reach 12. Start twisting them slowly to the right and back so that you go to 1, 2 and then 3. Stop for a few seconds at 3 and then move on to 6. The same way go on to 7, 8 and 9 (hold for a few seconds) and then on to 10, 11 and 12. That completes one rotation. Now do a similar slow rotation in the reverse direction. Counting that as one set, complete 20 sets in all.

Care has to be taken that this rotation must be done as slowly as possible, virtually at the speed of the clock's second hand. Unfortunately, you will find many people rotating their knees at a breakneck speed. Doing it quickly does more harm than good.

If bending is difficult for you, you can do the exercise without putting your palms on the knees. Instead, raise your hands to the shoulder level in front of you, look forward and then do the knee rotation.

Some prefer to do 20 clockwise rotations and then go on to 20 anti-clockwise ones, but it is better to change the direction every time. That is not only less tiring but also more beneficial.

Exercise No. 8:

This one is also for the knees. Put your palms on the knees or stand erect with hands in front at the shoulder level. Gently start bending down as if you are going to sit on a chair that is not there. When your thighs are parallel to the ground – stop and count up to 10. Slowly come back to the original position.

Care has to be taken that your thighs are parallel to the ground. If you bend too little, you do not get full benefit; go too far down and you put too much strain on your knees. Once your knees have become conditioned, it will be fine for you to go all the way down as if sitting on an Indian-style toilet but for the time being, confine yourself to making your thighs parallel to the ground.

Exercise No. 9:

We move up to the next joint. This, too, is very important because not only is it misused but it is also the spot where many people accumulate fat. Exercising it will benefit you both ways.

Put your palms on your hips. As in exercise 7, imagine that you are standing atop a clock. The 12 will be in front of you, 3 will be to your right, 6 will be behind you and 9 will be towards your left.

Take your hips to 12 first, and then rotate clockwise so that you reach 3, 6 and 9 like a second's hand. Do it gently and slowly. Remember, your feet are not moving, nor is your upper torso. Only the hips go through a complete rotation.

If you have not been exercising regularly, even these simple exercises will tire you out. There is nothing to worry about. You will regain breath soon enough. Soon you will become so adept that you will be able to finish all exercises effortlessly.

Week 10

Every living organism works best in a conducive environment. The fish needs water, human beings need air. Our cells and tissues function properly only when the alkaline-acidic balance of the body is right. To achieve this, we need 80 per cent of alkaline matter and 20 per cent of acidic matter from our foods. That means we should fill ourselves up with four-fifths of the foods that leave an alkaline imprint and one-fifth with acidic foods.

If the percentage of acidic foods goes up, to say 21 per cent, you will have mild acidity. The higher it goes, the more severe the acidity problem.

To understand this in a simpler way, think of your blended clothes. They normally have 80 per cent cotton and 20 per cent polyester. Experience has taught us that this combination works best.

If you wear pure nylon or terylene/acrylic clothes, you are bound to face several difficulties. They are hot in summers, cool in winters and if they come in contact with a spark of fire, you've had it! Not only that, they start smelling after you have worn them for a few hours.

We make quite similar dietary mistakes too. Instead of eating a diet, which comprises 80 per cent alkaline foods and 20 per cent acidic foods, we do something exactly the opposite. Out of innocence, we eat

80 per cent acidic food and only 20 per cent alkaline food. And then we crib that our heart, or lungs or the knees are not what they should be. How can they be, if you are feeding them something that is just not designed for them?

It is now time to restore the balance. All that you have to do is to gorge on alkaline foods and cut down acidic ones as much as possible. Believe me, that is easier than it sounds. You just have to know the broad distinction between what is alkaline and what is acidic.

Let's not go into listing each and every item that falls in this or that category. Knowing the general classification will suffice.

Let us begin with alkaline items. Almost all fruits are alkaline. The darker they are, the more alkaline they will be. So, berries like *jamuns* and cherries will be very alkaline, bananas will be a little less, but alkaline nevertheless.

The same is true of vegetables. Most of what we eat daily are in the alkaline category. Those that grow above the ground like tomatoes and peas are more alkaline; those growing below the ground like carrots or potatoes slightly less so, but it is all a matter of degree. Only those that are used in *masalas* – like onion and garlic – tend to be acidic.

Consequently, most of the fresh fruit and vegetable juices are alkaline. So are milk and curd. Milk, which is not too hot, is particularly alkaline.

Most of the dry fruits are alkaline as well. But here, some explanation is required. In everyday parlance, nuts like almonds, walnuts, pistachios or groundnuts are also counted as dry fruits, which they are not. When we say dry fruits, we mean those eatables like raisins or figs, which were fruits at one stage but have been dried so that they can be stored. So, it is these – dates, raisins, figs, and so on – that are alkaline.

The bad news is that the list of alkaline items has almost come to an end. Nearly all other eatables come into the acidic category. Grains are acidic, so is rice. Pulses and beans also fall in the same category. Meat, eggs, alcohol, tea, coffee are all the more so.

Yet, what is our staple diet? Many of us spend the whole life on a *roti-rice-dal* cycle. We either eat very little salad, or none at all. If at all we do eat it, we prefer onion, which is in the acidic category, along with garlic. The end result is that we are on a highly acidic track. A simple analogy will be that instead of putting two litres of petrol and a few millilitres of mobil-oil in the tank of our scooter, we are pouring in two litres of mobil-oil and just a few drops of petrol. Isn't the scooter going to be in deep trouble?

So what needs to be done? Here are a few simple diet modifications that will help you to restore the balance:

One, make it a habit to consume one to one and a half kilogram of fruits every day. You don't have to eat that much of a single fruit. Taking several different fruits is a far better option. So, you can have some apples, some grapes and some guavas if you like. As long as the total comes to one kilogram or so, you will be fine.

Those who have diabetes should avoid fruits not permissible to them, but others can take all fruits freely. Here I must mention that just because we are prohibited from eating fruits like grapes in diabetes, we think that they may the cause of diabetes. Nothing could be farther from the truth. It only means that we have overloaded our system so much that it cannot even handle regular fruits. That does not mean that the fruits themselves are the villains. Nothing made by nature harms us, until we take in excessive quantities of it.

Nor do you have to take all that bulk at one time. Snacking on them several times a day will take care of your needs. If you think that eating fruit is a chore, please remind yourself that it is much better than popping pills, isn't it?

Two, with every meal, make it a point to eat lots and lots of green salad. You can start with just a quarter-plate of salad. By and by, you may increase it to a full plate. When you are eating so much of greens, obviously you will be cutting down on your *chapattis* and rice. Soon the alkaline-acidic balance will be restored and you will start feeling much lighter. The amount of food that you eat will be the same; you will be only eating what is right for you.

Please remember that there is nothing wrong with acidic foods. In fact, we need the full 20 per cent of them. It is the excessive intake that is harmful. So do not decide to stop eating *chapattis* or rice or *dal*. They are your staple diet. It is just that we require four times as much fruits and vegetables too.

Three, suppose there is a *sabzi* as well as *dal* on your plate; normally, whenever we go for a second helping, we tend to take *dal*. Now make it a point to prefer *sabzi* as second helping. Even when cooked, *sabzi* is *sabzi* and it will go into your alkaline quota.

One wonderful feature of food items is that once they are sprouted, even acidic items turn alkaline. So, eat sprouts liberally. Pulses like black or green grams (*chana, moong*) and so on, make excellent sprouts. If you are fond of porridge, then go in for porridge made of sprouted wheat. It will be light and nutritious (sprouts are rich in digestible energy, bio-available vitamins, minerals, amino acids, proteins, beneficial enzymes and phytochemicals), and are alkaline.

One problem is that while sprouts are excellent for eating raw or steamed, they cannot be cooked into a *dal* because they tend to be become tasteless or even bitter. Here is a trick by which you can make *dal* out of sprouts, which tastes good and also counts among your alkaline food.

For eating raw, the best sprouts are the ones that have a long radicle (root) growing out of them. But these are useless for cooking. So when you soak *dal* for sprouting, separate those seeds which have just started sprouting and put them in the fridge or a cool place so that they don't sprout any further. These will be just right for making *dal* and will be alkaline as well. The character of the grains changes as soon as the sprouting process begins. You will only see a white dot trying to grow out of them.

This liberal intake of fruits and vegetables will be enough to bring a revolutionary change in your life. The results take some time to manifest, but are certain and amazing.

Waist and shoulder exercises

We move on to three new yoga exercises. As you add more and more of them every week, you may start running short of time. If you cannot fit them into the time available with you, please start reducing the number of repetitions but exercise each and every part of the body in the morning itself. Various joints should be considered as your close relatives living in a particular city. Whichever relative you do not pay a visit is going to get annoyed. So even if it is a brief visit, take care of them all.

Exercise No. 10:

Put your hands on your waist, thumbs forward and fingers towards the back. Bend at the waist to make a T shape. Now your head is at the spot 12. As in previous exercises, twist your waist in such a way that the head goes to 1, 2 and then 3. Stop there awhile, move on to 4 and 5 and then again stop longer at 6. In the same way go to 7, 8, 9 (stop) and 10, 11 and 12 to complete one rotation. Make the next rotation in the reverse direction. That makes one set. Do 20 sets in all.

Some may feel giddy on bending

forward. If that is the case with you, don't bend forward at 90 degrees but only at 45 degrees and then do the rotations.

If, initially, you find even that unmanageable, just bend forward and backwards 20 times and then bend towards left and right 20 times.

Please remember that this is only a temporary arrangement. Your final goal should be to do complete rotations.

Exercise No. 11:
This one is for your shoulders:

a) Stand erect and raise your shoulders upwards till they almost touch your ears. Fairly briskly, drop them downwards. Do at least 20 times and see yourself getting energised.
b) Rotate your left shoulder backwards 10 times as if it is the wheel of a car. Then rotate it forward 10 times.

c) Do exactly as in (b) with your right shoulder.
d) Now rotate both shoulders forward 10 times and backwards 10 times.

Exercise No. 12:

You must have seen children playing on the seesaw. In the same way, move your left shoulder upwards and the right shoulder downwards. Then reverse the shoulders. Make this seesaw motion at least 20 times.

Once you are through with that, rotate the shoulders backwards and forwards 10 times in such a way that at any given time the left shoulder is up and the right one is down. In the next rotation, the order will be reversed.

Week 11

The shift from predominantly acidic to alkaline food must have started bringing about a subtle transformation in your life. But the full results will take some time to manifest. For the time being, just follow it regularly and optimistically. You will be amazed at the benefits that will start flowing your way after a few weeks of persistence.

This week, we will talk about the time gap between meals. As you are well aware, our body needs energy on a constant basis. Even when we are sleeping, we require energy, although it is far less than what we need when we are walking or running.

To maintain this supply, we need to eat fairly often. In fact, we have to eat every 150 minutes or so for optimum utilisation of food. Yet, in most cultures we have the tradition of having three square meals a day: breakfast, lunch and dinner. We must understand why this custom of three meals was evolved.

In the bygone era, when food habits were being established, there was neither electricity nor cooking gas. Food was cooked over an open fire (*chulha or angithi*). Anybody who has used them knows that it is a backbreaking job to get the fire going, and even putting it off. The end result was that even for cooking just three meals, women had to spend virtually all their time in the kitchen. The hustle-bustle for breakfast would start around 6 am and go on till 10 am. The lunch preparation would start one hour later and it would be 3 pm by the time the table was cleared. An hour of rest and it would be time to start preparing for dinner. Phew!

Men also had to undergo a tough routine. It was an agrarian society and finding time to eat was a luxury. So, they too, preferred only three meals a day. The breakfast was taken early at home before rushing to the fields. The lady of the house would travel to the fields with the lunch. The dinner was eaten upon return.

By and by, electric and gas gadgets came in. Fridges and microwave ovens entered every household. It was time to shift to eating every two hours instead of four hours, which was the norm till then, but quite the opposite happened. People, especially in the North, went from three to just two meals. They had invented an abomination called the brunch (by combining breakfast and lunch). They would rather proudly announce that they leave home after having brunch and were so *disciplined* that would only have home-cooked food on return late in the evening.

And what about the mid-day hunger? Oh, nothing more than some *samosas* or bread *pakoras* or other such snacks. For them these were the fully acceptable items to satiate their hunger.

Nothing could be more damaging for the system. First of all, eating after a long gap was bad enough. It was like the traffic jam, which always takes place when all the office people come on to the street, all at the same time. Had they taken several small meals, it would have been fairly smooth sailing. But eating two or three big meals was the best way to ruin the digestive system.

To cap it all, the oily and fried items that were taken, further clogged the system. Unfortunately, that is the lifestyle many of us maintain.

From now on, please incorporate two or three mini-meals between your breakfast, lunch and dinner, so that you eat six to seven times a day and the gap between two meals is never more than two and a half hours.

Suppose you finish your breakfast at 9 am, lunch at 2 pm and dinner at 9 pm. Then you will require one snack session at 11:30 am, one at 4:30 pm and one at around 7 pm.

If there are times when you feel full midway through your breakfast; please set aside the leftovers for your next snack at 11:30 am. The same will be the case with your lunch. But even otherwise, here is a simple menu for your snacking time.

Your staple snack-time diet will be fresh fruits. After all, you have to polish off one to one and a half kilograms of fruit to maintain the acidic-alkaline balance. The snack time is the best time to consume them.

The other item on your menu will be vegetables. Any seasonal vegetable that you like – radish, carrots or cucumber – will be fine. These will be filling and will also not cause you any harm.

At times, you will be caught in such a situation that fruits and vegetables will just not be available. For such contingencies you should keep some dry fruits listed below ready in your house, in your car and in your office.

1. Dates (these days you get very good seedless ones and you can eat a few at any time)
2. *Chhuhare* (those who are not familiar with them should know that they are nothing more than dry dates. If you don't find them, no problem; the dates will do)
3. Raisins (*kishmish* are full of fibre and also pep you up)
4. *Munakka* (this is also only a variety of raisins. Raisins are sweet; *munakka* has a tangy taste. Raisins have no seeds, munakkas that come from sour grapes do have them.)
5. Dried figs
6. Dried plums
7. Dried apricots

8. Blueberries
9. Blackberries
10. Cranberries, and so on.

In fact, you can use any dry fruit that strikes your fancy.

As you can see, all these items are sweet. So if you are suffering from diabetes, you cannot enjoy them. But for others, they are absolutely fine. Don't worry, despite the sweet taste, they will neither cause diabetes nor add to your weight. We will talk about that subject in detail a little later.

As far as the quantity is concerned, your day's quota should not go beyond about a teacupful of dry fruits. You can fill the cup with either one of these items or several of them. If you chew them properly, you just cannot have too much of them. But even if you do, they will not cause much damage, as your biscuits or bread-*pakoras* do.

Perhaps you require some savouries too. Why not? Roasted *papads, chanas* and soyabean make excellent savoury snacks. In fact, most good stores stock a vast variety of roasted *namkeens* these days. Make full use of them.

Once your system knows that it will require to eat some more just two and a half hours later, it will demand only limited food at breakfast and lunch. When it knows that you are going to be hungry for the next four hours or more, it tends to gobble up much more than what it can handle.

In fact, it has been noticed that most overeating is done at the time of dinner. That is the time when most people get to eat leisurely with their family and they tend to over-indulge. The best remedy for that problem is the 7 pm snack. If you are not voraciously hungry at 9, you are not going to eat too much at the dinner table, even if family members force you to.

Please try to finish your dinner at least two hours before sleep time. Lying down soon after dinner makes you put on weight.

Serious bingeing does not take place at home but at parties. It is a pity that at most such gatherings, the dinner is served no earlier than 10.30 pm. Before that, there are an endless variety of snacks to tempt you. Since guests are hungry and are idle, they tend to overeat. If you leave for such parties after taking your snacks at 7 pm, it is certain that you are not going to eat in excess there.

All of us have to attend some dinners only as a formality. At these, most tend to eat bad food in excess for several subconscious reasons. One, they want to avoid eating at home at least for that day. Two, they think that since they have spent so much on giving *shagun* at the party, they might as well eat their fill.

It is time to shed this attitude. Please remind yourself that I am not quite so impoverished that I have to eat at others' places. I am in a position to feed others if need be. Why should I be keen to eat at someone else's house? Also, the money given as *shagun* is already wasted. At least I should not spoil my health by eating what I normally would not have at home.

Since we have had a rich dinner and that too late in the night, we don't feel hungry in the morning. After all, the undigested food is still sitting there. So, we tend to skip breakfast. Please don't! The old adage that one should breakfast like a king, have lunch like a prince and dinner like a beggar is more relevant today than ever before. Turning this adage upside down would harm only us.

Even if you are eating at home, use the dinnertime as audit time. The bank cashiers balance debit and credit columns every day. In the same way, ask yourself an honest question at dinnertime: do I really need the full meal? Your inner voice may tell you that only soup and salad are enough for you. Live on that. Maybe, you don't need anything more than a glass of milk after having had a healthy snack at 7.30. Please don't go beyond that limit.

Even if hunger pangs strike you at midnight, do not make a clandestine visit to the fridge. Bear the hunger for one day and soon enough the 12 am hunger will subside and you will start needing your breakfast regularly.

Also, do not force anyone to eat more than what he really wants. You will only be completing a formality, but someone may get browbeaten into crossing their limits and then repent later.

One healthy development is that at most parties, now it has become virtually mandatory to place several salads near the central table where dinner plates are stored. If you don't feel like it, please don't go to the main stall at all. These salads will fill you sufficiently.

Don't worry, the host won't mind. Even if he says, *"Arrey aap ne to kuchh liya hi nahin!"* ("You haven't eaten anything!"), he will be doing so only for formality's sake. Soon your reputation that you are a sensible eater would spread and nobody would force you. Friends may be outwardly ribbing you, but in their heart of hearts, they will be admiring you. Please remember, whatever the pressure people put on you to eat extra, nobody really likes a glutton.

Three cheers to sensible eating!

Exercising your neck
After the shoulder exercises last week, it is time to move to your neck. Be particularly careful while doing these exercises, and avoid jerks because the neck is a very sensitive part of our body.

Exercise No. 13:
Sit erect. Gently bring your head down so that your chin touches the neck. Your head is now at position 12. Rotate the neck so that it goes to all the extremities,

stopping at 3, which will be when the right ear is almost touching your right shoulder, 6 when the head will be tilted backwards to the maximum extent possible, and 9 when the left ear is touching the left shoulder. Coming back to the front will complete one rotation. Make the next neck rotation anticlockwise. This way, make 20 rotations in all.

Doing it slowly is very important. Twist the neck in all directions completely.

If you suffer from neck pain, do not bend the neck forward fully, but you can rotate the neck in every other direction as described earlier.

Exercise No. 14:

Bend the neck forward as much as possible and then bend it backwards, again as much as possible. Do so 20 times.

After that, do another variation. Bend the neck forward, then backward. When the neck is totally tilted backward, open your mouth wide, as if you are going to eat a big *laddu* (Indian ball-shaped sweet). Once the sweetmeat is in your mouth, open and close your mouth several times as if you are masticating the *laddu*. See how it affects your chin. Repeat 20 times, each time opening and closing your mouth at least thrice.

Now, instead of opening and closing your mouth when the neck is tilted backwards, simply make a beak out of your lips, as if you are trying to kiss the sky. Repeat 20 times, each time making a beak thrice. Again watch the effect of the exercise on the front and the back of the neck.

Exercise No. 15:

Tilt your neck left and right so that your left ear touches the left shoulder first and then the right ear touches the right shoulder. Do not raise the shoulders. The movement should be from the neck. Repeat 20 times on each side.

These neck exercises and some others, which will be described next week, should be done whenever you have sat in one posture for too long, whether it is when you are driving or typing or reading or playing a video game.

Week 12

So far, we have banished two enemies from our diet: *maida* and *khoya* (or *mawa*). This week, we will get rid of our third major adversary. It is none other than sugar. The white poison should be counted more dangerous than alcohol or heroin, because when you drink or take drugs, you are at least aware that you are harming yourself. Sugar on the other hand is a silent killer because very few know its lethal, real nature.

The best that most know is that it causes tooth decay and also can contribute to diabetes. (In fact, some do not even believe that the eating of sugar causes diabetes. But the bitter truth is that besides these diseases, sugar actually causes hundreds of others as well.)

These innocuous white crystals play havoc with your body, heart as well as mind. There is not a disease in which sugar is not a contributing factor. It has two things in abundance: taste and calories. The downside is that it has got nothing positive at all: no nutrients, no fibre, no minerals, no fats and no enzymes.

If it is taken in moderation, it may not cause much harm. But moderation in this case only means as much of sugar in a day as you take salt: about half a teaspoon. Unfortunately, most of us consume 10, 20 or even 30 times as much, day in and day out. That overload makes it nothing less than sweet poison.

Yet, its consumption increases and increases exponentially because it is an addictive substance. The more you eat, the more you crave. Secondly, it seems to give the consumer a sort of a high. That is why farmhands are still encouraged to eat a lot of *gur* (jaggery) before they begin a hard day's work. But what most do not know is that the high is followed by a low. When that comes, we either have to eat more of it, or feel run down.

That happens because loads of calcium, sodium, potassium and magnesium have to be taken from various parts of the body to digest the sugar. The body falls short of these chemicals. That results in everything from osteoporosis to the failure of the body to get rid of poisonous residues.

It is almost a drug like heroin and is still used as a food item of everyday use, thereby ruining the health of innocent millions.

The more sugar you eat, the more you raise the level of insulin in your blood. Insulin in turn stores fat, a risk factor of diabetes, and can damage artery walls, and makes it easier for cholesterol and fat to build up and cause heart disease.

It is particularly bad for obese people because even a spoonful of sugar in a day is enough to add to their weight.

Glutamic acid is essential for orderly functioning of our brain. Sugar consumption kills those bacteria in the intestines that manufacture B vitamin complex. When the level of B vitamin complex falls, the glutamic acid is not produced, leading to sleepiness. A high level of sugar in the blood leads to a confused state of mind, and even an unsound mind. So it can cause everything from mood swings, personality changes, increased chances of depression, nervous disorders and anxiety to hypertension and stress.

Nancy Appleton, PhD, has compiled a detailed list of 145 diseases that it causes, which should be self-explanatory and an eye-opener. The scientific studies that have reached these conclusions after extensive research are mentioned at the end. Here goes the long list:

1. Sugar can suppress the immune system.
2. Sugar upsets the mineral relationships in the body.
3. Sugar can cause hyperactivity, anxiety, difficulty in concentrating, and crankiness in children.
4. Sugar can produce a significant rise in triglycerides.
5. Sugar contributes to the reduction in defence against bacterial infection (infectious diseases).
6. Sugar causes a loss of tissue elasticity and function, the more sugar you eat the more elasticity and function you lose.
7. Sugar reduces high-density lipoproteins.
8. Sugar leads to chromium deficiency.
9. Sugar leads to cancer of the ovaries.
10. Sugar can increase fasting levels of glucose.
11. Sugar causes copper deficiency.
12. Sugar interferes with absorption of calcium and magnesium.
13. Sugar can weaken eyesight.
14. Sugar raises the level of the neurotransmitters: dopamine, serotonin, and norepinephrine.
15. Sugar can cause hypoglycaemia.
16. Sugar can produce an acidic digestive tract.
17. Sugar can cause a rapid rise of adrenaline levels in children.
18. Sugar malabsorption is frequent in patients with functional bowel disease.
19. Sugar can cause premature ageing.
20. Sugar can lead to alcoholism.
21. Sugar can cause tooth decay.
22. Sugar contributes to obesity
23. High intake of sugar increases the risk of Crohn's disease, and ulcerative colitis.
24. Sugar can cause changes frequently found in person with gastric or duodenal ulcers.
25. Sugar can cause arthritis.

26. Sugar can cause asthma.
27. Sugar greatly assists the uncontrolled growth of Candida Albicans (yeast infections).
28. Sugar can cause gallstones.
29. Sugar can cause heart disease.
30. Sugar can cause appendicitis.
31. Sugar can cause multiple sclerosis.
32. Sugar can cause haemorrhoids.
33. Sugar can cause varicose veins.
34. Sugar can elevate glucose and insulin responses in oral contraceptive users.
35. Sugar can lead to periodontal disease.
36. Sugar can contribute to osteoporosis.
37. Sugar contributes to saliva acidity.
38. Sugar can cause a decrease in insulin sensitivity.
39. Sugar can lower the amount of Vitamin E (alpha-Tocopherol in the blood).
40. Sugar can decrease growth hormone.
41. Sugar can increase cholesterol.
42. Sugar can increase the systolic blood pressure.
43. Sugar can cause drowsiness and decreased activity in children.
44. High sugar intake increases advanced glycation end products (AGEs) (Sugar bound non-enzymatically to protein)
45. Sugar can interfere with the absorption of protein.
46. Sugar causes food allergies.
47. Sugar can contribute to diabetes.
48. Sugar can cause toxaemia during pregnancy.
49. Sugar can contribute to eczema in children.
50. Sugar can cause cardiovascular disease.
51. Sugar can impair the structure of DNA.
52. Sugar can change the structure of protein.
53. Sugar can make our skin age by changing the structure of collagen.
54. Sugar can cause cataracts.

55. Sugar can cause emphysema.
56. Sugar can cause atherosclerosis.
57. Sugar can promote an elevation of low-density lipoproteins (LDL).
58. High sugar intake can impair the physiological homeostasis of many systems in the body.
59. Sugar lowers the enzymes' ability to function.
60. Sugar intake is higher in people with Parkinson's disease.
61. Sugar can cause a permanent alteration of the way that proteins act in the body.
62. Sugar can increase the size of the liver by making the liver cells divide.
63. Sugar can increase the amount of liver fat.
64. Sugar can increase kidney size and produce pathological changes in the kidney.
65. Sugar can damage the pancreas.
66. Sugar can increase the body's fluid retention.
67. Sugar is enemy no. 1 of bowel movements.
68. Sugar can cause myopia (nearsightedness).
69. Sugar can compromise the lining of the capillaries.
70. Sugar can make the tendons more brittle.
71. Sugar can cause headaches, including migraine.
72. Sugar plays a role in pancreatic cancer in women.
73. Sugar can adversely affect school children's grades and cause learning disorders.
74. Sugar can cause an increase in delta, alpha, and theta brain waves.
75. Sugar can cause depression.
76. Sugar increases the risk of gastric cancer.
77. Sugar can cause dyspepsia (indigestion).
78. Sugar can increase your risk of getting gout.
79. Sugar can increase the levels of glucose in an oral glucose tolerance test.
80. Sugar can increase the insulin responses in humans consuming high-sugar diets when compared to humans on low sugar diets.

81. Highly refined sugar diet reduces learning capacity.
82. Sugar can cause less effective functioning of two blood proteins, albumin and lipoproteins, which may reduce the body's ability to handle fat and cholesterol.
83. Sugar can contribute to Alzheimer's disease.
84. Sugar can cause platelet adhesiveness.
85. Sugar can cause hormonal imbalance; some hormones become underactive and others become overactive.
86. Sugar can lead to the formation of kidney stones.
87. Sugar can lead to the hypothalamus to become highly sensitive to a large variety of stimuli.
88. Sugar can lead to dizziness.
89. Diets high in sugar can cause free radicals and oxidative stress.
90. High sucrose diets of subjects with peripheral vascular disease significantly increase platelet adhesion.
91. A high sugar diet can lead to biliary tract cancer.
92. Sugar feeds cancer.
93. High sugar consumption of pregnant adolescents is associated with a twofold increased risk for delivering a small-for-gestational-age (SGA) infant.
94. High sugar consumption can lead to substantial decrease in gestation duration among adolescents.
95. Sugar slows food's travel time through the gastrointestinal tract.
96. Sugar increases the concentration of bile acids in stools and bacterial enzymes in the colon. This can modify bile to produce cancer-causing compounds and colon cancer.
97. Sugar increases estradiol (the most potent form of naturally occurring estrogen) in men.
98. Sugar combines and destroys phosphatase, an enzyme, which makes the process of digestion more difficult.
99. Sugar can be a risk factor of gallbladder cancer.
100. Sugar is an addictive substance.
101. Sugar can be intoxicating, similar to alcohol.
102. Sugar can exacerbate pre-menstrual syndrome (PMS).

103. Sugar given to premature babies can affect the amount of carbon dioxide they produce.
104. Decrease in sugar intake can increase emotional stability.
105. The body changes sugar into two -five times more fat in the bloodstream than it does starch.
106. The rapid absorption of sugar promotes excessive food intake in obese subjects.
107. Sugar can worsen the symptoms of children with attention deficit hyperactivity disorder (ADHD).
108. Sugar adversely affects urinary electrolyte composition.
109. Sugar can slow down the ability of the adrenal glands to function.
110. Sugar has the potential of inducing abnormal metabolic processes in a normal healthy individual and to promote chronic degenerative diseases.
111. Intravenous feeding (IVs) of sugar water can cut off oxygen to the brain.
112. A high sucrose intake could be an important risk factor in lung cancer.
113. Sugar increases the risk of polio.
114. High sugar intake can cause epileptic seizures.
115. Sugar causes high blood pressure in obese people.
116. In Intensive Care Units, limiting sugar saves lives.
117. Sugar may induce cell death.
118. Sugar can increase the amount of food that you eat.
119. In juvenile rehabilitation camps, when children were put on a low sugar diet, there was a 44% drop in antisocial behaviour.
120. Sugar can lead to prostrate cancer.
121. Sugar dehydrates newborns. Correct the numbering after this
122. Sugar can cause low birth of babies with low birth-weight.
123. Greater consumption of refined sugar is associated with a worsened outcome of schizophrenia.
124. Sugar can raise homocysteine levels in the blood stream.
125. Sweet food items increase the risk of breast cancer.
126. Sugar is a risk factor in cancer of the small intestine.

127. Sugar may cause laryngeal cancer.
128. Sugar induces salt and water retention.
129. Sugar may contribute to mild memory loss.
130. As sugar increases in the diet of 10 years olds, there is a linear decrease in the intake of many essential nutrients.
131. Sugar can increase the total amount of food consumed.
132. Exposing a newborn to sugar results in a heightened preference for sucrose relative to water at six months and two years of age.
133. Sugar causes constipation.
134. Sugar causes varicose veins.
135. Sugar can cause brain decay in prediabetic and diabetic women.
136. Sugar can increase the risk of stomach cancer.
137. Sugar can cause metabolic syndrome.
138. Sugar ingestion by pregnant women increases neural tube defects in embryos.
139. Sugar can be a factor in asthma.
140. The higher the sugar consumption the more chances of getting irritable bowel syndrome.
141. Sugar could affect central reward systems.
142. Sugar can cause cancer of the rectum.
143. Sugar can cause endometrial cancer.
144. Sugar can cause renal (kidney) cell carcinoma.
145. Sugar can cause liver tumours.

I suggest that you read this list faithfully every morning. If you feel like acquiring any of these diseases, do succumb to your cravings. Otherwise, banish this white poison from your kitchen cupboard.

As the list makes it abundantly clear, there is not a disease under the sun to which sugar does not contribute. If you find the list of 145 diseases too long, just read those that have been given in bold letters. These are the diseases that are fairly well known to even laymen. Sugar is the culprit in the onset of all of these.

I draw your special attention to serial number 100: sugar is an addictive substance, and once you are hooked on to it, it is quite difficult to free yourself from its clutches. But free you must get.

If you quit it all of a sudden, there are bound to be withdrawal symptoms. So cut down sugar gradually. Supposing you put two spoons of sugar in your cup of tea at present. Bring the quantity down to one and three-quarters to begin with. Let the body get attuned and then reduce some more.

Soon you will realise that you were unnecessarily pouring in sugar into various items, even those that have natural sweetness. For instance, milk is full of natural sugar. In fact, wheat and rice also have sugary elements. That is why those with diabetes cannot eat even these items. But those who are disease-free can get their quota of sugar from these items.

Plus, I have already recommended that you eat some dry fruits, all of which happen to be sweet. Once you cut down on table sugar, the natural sugar that you get from those dry fruits will take care of all your bodily needs.

Some people think that they can escape if they replace table sugar with jaggery or *shakkar*. Unfortunately, the digestive system cannot distinguish between the two. Yes, you can get some essential minerals from jaggery, but the harmful effects of jaggery will be as serious as that of sugar.

You must also be careful about hidden sugar. Many of sauces and ketchups are full of it. So are most of cola drinks. Tomato sauce has 23.6 per cent sugar, corn cereals eight per cent. Sugar sits hidden in fruit juice drinks, flavoured yoghurt, salad dressings etc. A 300-ml bottle of a cola drink may have as many as 11 teaspoons of sugar. Say a firm goodbye to all of them. Like Trojan's horse, the sugar in them is entering our system and wrecking it from the inside.

Why, even honey is not blame-free. It will cause the same complications as table sugar if you use it as a sweetening agent. That is why the bear is one animal that can suffer from tooth decay as well as diabetes. If one teaspoon of it is taken as a medicine, it is passable, but you cannot have it as replacement for sugar.

Some do give up sugar but get hooked to artificial sweetening agents. The problem is that many of those are carcinogenic, meaning thereby that they can cause cancer. Beware of them. If at all you have to patronize them, go in for those based on natural substances like stevia and xylitol.

More on neck care
It's exercise time now and we return to taking care of our neck, which is a problem area for many sedentary workers:

Exercise No. 16:
Sit or stand straight, looking forward. Now start twisting your neck to the left as if you are trying to look at someone sitting behind your left shoulder. Go to the extreme and hold. Count slowly up to 10 and then return to the starting position.

Now in the same manner, turn your neck towards the right, hold for a count of 10 and return to the starting position. This way, alternately turn the neck to left and right 20 times in all. Do this slowly and without any jerks.

Exercise No. 17:
Clasp your fingers as if you are getting ready to play volleyball. Put the clasped hands thumb-side on your forehead and turn your elbows sideways. Try to push your forehead forward while using the hands to stop it from moving. You

will notice the strain being felt in various parts of the neck while the force thus generated by the head will also strengthen your arms. Hold for as long as you can. Relax and then do it again.

Now take the hands to the back of the head. This time the last, little finger will be touching the head. Push your head backwards while you use your hands to make sure that it does not move backwards. Hold for as long as possible. Relax and repeat.

This way, do 20 repetitions in all, two forwards and two backwards.

Exercise No. 18:
Put your left hand on your left cheek, and point your elbow outwards. It will appear that you are trying to slap your left cheek.

Now try to turn your head to the left while using your hand to not let it move at all. Notice that certain other parts of the neck are being exercised. Hold for as long as you can. Relax and then do it again.

Now repeat the same exercise twice towards the right, by putting your right hand on your right cheek.

This way, do 20 repetitions in all, two towards the left and two towards the right. In other words, exert the force twice towards the left, and twice towards the right every time.

Week 13

Congratulations. You have already won 75 per cent of the battle. Now you are in the week when you can complete the triumph by becoming aware of the fourth and last enemy. After that you will only have to bother about a few minor adversaries and then get down to the task of repairing the damage done by hobnobbing with them, unwittingly, in the past.

But before you get down to brass tacks, here is a simple question for you. Suppose there are three glasses of water with you. You pour some table salt in one of them, a chunk of rock salt in the next and some finely powdered table salt packed in totally waterproof polythene bag in the third. Then you stir all three vigorously. Which one of them will take the longest to dissolve in the water?

If your answer is the third glass (table salt packed in polythene), then you are absolutely right. Had it not been covered in waterproof material, it would have dissolved in a jiffy. But since it is in an impermeable cover, it will not come in contact with water molecules and will thus sit there, almost forever.

That was just to illustrate a peculiarity of your digestive system. Food that cannot come in contact with the billions of microvilli inside the intestine cannot get digested. In other words, if you consume food covered in waterproof covering, it will just sit there.

In fact, drug smugglers make use of this characteristic. They consume several waterproof capsules containing drugs before going across a border. The drugs do not show when they are passing the enforcement agencies. Once they reach their destination, they pass the capsules out, clean them, open them and sell the stuff. Grotesque, but effective!

However, in normal circumstances, nobody takes food covered in a waterproof shell, right? No, wrong. We may not know it but that is what we do most of the time.

What happens is that the oil or ghee or fat we use to cook food makes a thin film around the food and renders it immune to the normal process of digestion. Result? Food, which should have been digested in a jiffy, takes interminably long to do so.

Since we are not aware of it, we accuse an innocent food-item to be hard to digest. As you know, those who have put on weight, deprive themselves of rice, potatoes and bananas, and so on. The fact of the matter is that these food-items do not make you fat (provided you do not overeat). But add fat to these items and they can be a killer. Potatoes would be a health food if eaten boiled or baked or microwaved. But when these are made into chips with the help of fat, they become that dreaded item which spends two minutes on the lips and two years on the hips!

In other words, if you can defeat this fourth and last enemy, you will be able to enjoy rice and potatoes freely. Rather, you will be able to enjoy many other items also.

Many argue that they take very little fat in any case. They are right but it is such an enemy that even a spoonful of it can make a film around a lot of food. So, that boiled rice that you had is perfectly fine, but the moment you fried it in a bit of oil, you have had it. The effect may not show immediately on those who are perfectly healthy but it can be telling on those who are weak, ailing or fat.

You must have seen people from the mosquito elimination programme going around pools of stagnant water during the rainy season with a can of black oil. Wherever they see any puddle, they pour a few drops of oil on the water. What happens is that mosquito larvae growing in such water have to come to the surface to breathe. Even a few drops of oil are enough to make a small film over water standing in a room-size area. The larvae cannot take air due the film and die.

In the same way, even a little bit of oil is enough to make a similar film around your food. Our endeavour is that till your health is fully recovered, you will not eat food in such a form that it will put an additional burden on your system.

Fortunately for us, people have become conscious of the ill effects of fat and they no longer pour as much ghee into their *dal* or *sabzi* as they used to do two or three decades back (in fact, old timers will recall that it was pretty common in villages to mix half a bowl of pure ghee (clarified butter) with an equal quantity of castor sugar and eat it as dessert. It was called *ghee-boora*. Such ghee-laden items are now on their way out, mercifully. Enlightened people now mostly use it only for frying.

Let us admit it, not many of us can have boiled food for too long. Our palate pines for the regular *dal-sabzi* after a few days of abstinence. I can never forget what happened to a promising cricketer from Haryana some years ago, whose bowling was so good that he was expected to make it to the national team. To help him occupy his rightful place, some friends and admirers of his got him a county contract in England. Everyone was convinced that after his stint there, he would be in the reckoning for donning the Indian Cap.

But he left his contract midway and returned home. Asked why, he said he could not survive without the *desi dal-sabzi*. Such is the lure of Indian-style cooking. For the benefit of such people, I shall describe a technique of frying almost every item, but without using ghee or oil. Incredible but true!

So how do you fry your food? It may be that you heat a few spoons of ghee in the container. When it starts crackling, you put onions, and so on, in it and fry till golden brown. Maybe, you then put in the other condiments. When the *masala* is done, you pour the vegetables, water, *haldi* (turmeric powder), salt and pepper and so on, and then bring the *sabzi* to a boil.

Simply replace ghee with tomato puree, which you can either make fresh by running tomatoes through the blender, or buy it readymade. Where you use one spoon of ghee or oil, you will need to use two spoons of tomato puree. And where the ghee used to be ready for putting in onions after one minute, the tomato puree will require two minutes (twice as long as fat) because of the water content in it. After that it will show the same characteristics as fat and you will have totally oil-free food.

Except for a few dishes like fried *karela* (bitter gourd) and *bhindi* (okra), you can make virtually everything this way. The taste will be very similar to dishes made while using oil and most people won't be able to tell the difference. But even if they do, you have the added advantage of satisfying their taste buds by pouring a bit of desi ghee over it after it has been cooked oil-free. In fact, ghee put this way makes *dal* and *sabzi* taste better. That it also spoils the health is another matter. But I am concerned only about your health. If others are keen to ruin their health, who are we to stop them?

Soon, you will start enjoying this kind of food so much that you will dread eating at places where food is cooked the conventional way. And since you will also enjoy the miracle of good health, you will wonder how in the world could you eat all that oil in the past?

Some well meaning but ill-informed friends might tell you that it is essential to take some amount of oil for good health. Please remember that almost all food items that we eat have oil in them. Wheat has wheat germ oil; corn oil is well known. Why, even the husk of rice yields rice bran oil. All these are sufficient to take care of your needs. The problem is that most people do not chew their food and that is why they cannot get the essential oils from their cereals. But since the very first chapter of this book requested you to start chewing food, you will not suffer from this problem.

Plus, you will now start eating nuts like almonds, cashews, walnuts and pistachios. They are full of oil, which is 100 times better than the extracted oil that many take.

While on the subject of nuts, let me add a word of caution about groundnuts. They are as beneficial as almonds, but since they are quite inexpensive, we tend to go overboard, and end up eating them in excess. Then they cause all sorts of problems. Please eat only as many groundnuts as you would eat almonds. Most people eat 5 to 10 almonds; so do not eat more of groundnuts. You will be able to enjoy their benefits without burdening your system.

Perhaps the practice of using so much oil in cooking started because people were not chewing their food and were thus depriving themselves of an essential ingredient. The shortage of oil was taken care of, but it led to many complications. Now the time has come to get good oil from nuts.

As said a little earlier, our endeavour is to come to zero oil use for these 20 weeks. After that, if you feel like, you can use a bit of it especially in items like *bhindi* and *karela*. If your system is totally clear, the use of this much of oil will be bearable. But when the alimentary canal is clogged, then even a teaspoon of it can be dangerous.

When you have to use fat, stick to monounsaturated fats, which come through oils like olive oil or cornola, but steer clear of *vanaspati ghee* (hydrogenated vegetable oils). This ghee, which is in solid state at room temperature, is far more dangerous than oil and pure ghee (clarified butter) because during the process of hydrogenation, many dangerous compounds are generated in it.

More on the neck, and then your shoulders

Exercise No. 19:
To start with, you bend your left knee. Bend your left knee at 90 degrees so that the wrist is totally horizontal. Put your bent hand near your navel. Keep the fully bent right elbow on top of it while your right palm is under your chin, fingers pointing forward.

Try to bend your neck downwards, while at the same time putting resistance with your right palm so that it cannot move down. Hold for as long as possible and then release the pressure. Repeat once again.

Now change hands, so that the right hand is down and the left elbow rests on it, while the left palm is under the chin. Try to bend the neck downwards, while making the left palm stop it. Release the pressure. Repeat.

You will notice that you are generating considerable force with your chin. But it is not being allowed to go waste. Instead, it is being used to strengthen your hands. So your neck and your hands are getting the much-need stimulation.

Exercise No. 20:

Stretch your hands sideways at shoulder height. Bend them so that your fingers touch your shoulders, while the elbows are pointed towards the left and the right. Now rotate your bent hands like the propeller of an aeroplane taking care that the elbows make as big circles as possible. Rotate 10 times in clockwise direction and 10 times in an anticlockwise direction.

When the elbows are at the highest position, they should be as close to your head as possible. Imagine that you are showing your elbows to God above, and you will be doing it just right.

Exercise No. 21:

Now rotate the elbows in such a manner that when the left elbow is at its highest, the right elbow is at its lowest. Repeat 10 times clockwise. Then change direction (rotate them anti-clockwise).

If you stop after each exercise and rest with eyes closed, and keep your attention remains focused inwards, this physical exertion will give your spiritual benefits also.

Week 14

You have emerged victorious over all major adversaries. You need not worry too much about the minor ones, although it will help if this week you take care of two others which are not in the same league as the four white snakes that you already slayed, but are still fairly venomous in their own right.

A considerably dangerous white killer is the seemingly innocuous table salt. God knows how many people have sent their blood pressure soaring due to excess of salt in their diet. Try to keep it under check as much as possible. That does not mean you have to totally eliminate it. That will lead to even bigger problems. Just don't go overboard.

The same is the case with tea and coffee. Caffeine in them has already got Bad Press and I need not dwell any more on that subject. Please also remember that tea has another compound called tannin, which ends up giving you many problems. Tannin can interfere with the absorption of iron, leading to several complications. Similarly, those with osteoporosis should either not take tea at all or take it in very limited quantity.

Some researchers like Julia Morton, a botanist on the staff of the University of Miami, have expressed fears after 24 years of research that tannin found in tea and red wine can cause cancer of the oesophagus (the muscle-membrane gullet that extends from the pharynx to the stomach). The tannin in black tea can be very harmful for the digestive system. So, please go in for green tea instead.

Caffeine can be released in less than two minutes. Tannin comes out in about three minutes. So, bagged tea is the best.

At least do not have tea and coffee early in the morning. On an empty stomach, they are at their most lethal. And until you have learnt to break the tea/coffee addiction, protect yourself by drinking extra water.

Beyond that, you don't have to bother about any other item. Feel free to eat everything, as long as you don't do so in excess. Your system is so powerful that it can handle virtually anything. It is only the *maida, khoya*, sugar and fat which make it helpless.

What they do to you need not be explained to those who are not willing to get rid of them, but since you have displayed the necessary determination, I am going to reveal the full extent of the havoc that they cause.

There are three kinds of problems: short term, medium term and long term. Let us go over them one by one.

The short-term effect can be felt the very next day. You will wake up sluggish, listless and heavy the day after consuming the white snakes. Once that day is over, you will feel that you have atoned for your dietary sins. But worse is yet to come, as a medium-term effect.

You will appear to be as good as normal on Day 3 and may be alright also on Day 4. But come Day 5 and you will wake up energy-less and sleepy, despite having had a full night's sleep. Your head may be aching or if you have a history of having body pain: a neckache or backache and it will get aggravated on this day. In fact, pain that you may have had in any body part in the past will suddenly flare up.

Worse, you will have a spoilt mood. You will be either excessively aggressive or unreasonably sad. Either way, you will tend to over-react. So, the *samosa* (which has *maida* as well as *ghee*) or the *jalebi* (which has *maida, ghee* and sugar) on Sunday will ruin your Thursday.

Another impact will be that suddenly you will have a boil or rash or eruption on your face. In fact, even the acne that the teenagers have is the result of wrong eating. If it was only because of hormonal changes, then even those areas and countries where the diet is not so rich would have had them.

To remember the rule, just look at your hand. Your thumb comprises the day you ate wrong items. The index finger represents the next day when you will feel slightly heavy. The middle and ring fingers represent the two days when you will feel that it wasn't a bad bargain after all to have enjoyed all those items because on these days you will be as good as normal with no effects of the binge on Day 1. And the little finger stands for the fifth day when the medium-term effect of your indulgence will hit you the hardest.

If you are used to eating such items on a daily basis, you may face one or more of these problems regularly, and won't even know a better life. Only those who have kept away from the four snakes for some time will know what I am talking about. I have helped countless people cure their migraine merely by stopping these four items.

The difficulty is that people do not associate bad health with bad eating. Those few who do see the correlation think that the upset stomach or the headache that they are having is because of what they ate the previous night. This wrong notion leads to many misunderstandings. Suppose someone wakes up on Tuesday morning with a headache. He will invariably say that it is because of what he ate the previous night. So he will start racking his brains about the dinner menu. If it is tomatoes that he ate in abundance the previous night, he will convince himself that tomatoes do not agree with him. If it is *khichdi* or porridge, even these will be castigated as too dangerous, whereas the blame actually may lie with the *rasgullas* that he polished off five days ago.

So how should you put this rule of the hand to good use? There are three ways. One, when you know that you have a big event coming on Thursday next, make sure that you eat none of the taboo items after Sunday. Ideally, you should not eat them ever, but if at all you do, at least stop eating those items four or five days before the programme.

Secondly, when you end up eating the food that you should not have, make a note of the date on which this mistake was made. When the fifth day arrives, steel yourself and do not brood over anyone's faults at all. On the day in question, you would be hyper-sensitive. Even manageable difficulties would appear to be unbearable. You will not only feel cross with whatever is said or done to you, you will also blame everyone for your never-ending woes.

The third 'good use' is being revealed to you only in jest; do not actually practice it. When you get to know that your rival has something major lined up for Thursday – an exam, a party or a celebration, may be – just call him over for a lavish lunch or dinner on Sunday. Wine and dine him well. He will be praising you, but when the big day comes, he will be down in the dumps. Food can be that lethal!

The tragedy is that we are not done yet. The long-term effect will manifest itself many years later and may include anything from the long list of 145 ailments associated with sugar, plus many other diseases like blood pressure, spondylitis, heart problem and even cancer. It is just that these lifestyle diseases take decades in the making, so no one does anything to prevent them.

You must have heard of many instances of people drinking themselves or smoking themselves to death. But I am sure you cannot quote even one example where someone died of drinking or smoking in a day or even a month. The human body is so sturdy that it resists the effect of these poisons for decades. The consequences of consuming *maida*, *khoya*, sugar and fat may take even longer to manifest, but they hit you for sure. Wake up as early as you can.

Since you have banished the four enemies, now is the time to wipe out their ill effects. You must realise that whatever we eat has only two destinations: ideally, most of it should get converted into energy and the waste material should be quickly expelled from the body. Unfortunately when you were eating these unhealthy items, there were twin problems. One, they were not getting converted into energy properly and, two, they were generating waste material which was so stubborn that it was very difficult, if not impossible, to eliminate. As this garbage accumulated, it caused all sorts of problems. Once it increases beyond a certain level, it can even kill you.

Trying to eliminate them would have been pointless when you were still eating them. Now that you have banished them, it is time to launch a thorough cleaning. After all, we cannot wait for years to open up the clogged pipes. We will try to do so within six months. The more you reduce the toxicity, the healthier you will become.

It is slow, patient work. After all, toxins accumulated over so many years cannot be wished away by any magic. We should be thankful to Nature that the mayhem caused by decades of leading a "lavish" lifestyle can be undone in a matter of months.

A wonderful feature of the body is that whenever it is given some rest, it starts repairing itself. When the digestive system is relieved of its daily chore of digesting food somewhat, it settles down to conducting the self-healing exercise.

In fact, the custom of being on a fast at least once a month – if not once a week – was started for this very purpose. Unfortunately, because of our own mistakes, the fasting period is now the time when we get upset stomachs most often, for the simple reason that we have started eating junk food aplenty during this period. The fast is started with heavy eatables and is ended also with such items. This plays havoc with the system. Now, the time has come for you to give some genuine rest to your system once every week. We will prepare your system gradually so that it can make do with lesser and lesser food items.

Reserve one day as the rest period. Picking a day at random – let it be Wednesday. So, this coming Wednesday, please eliminate all lentils from your food and also all milk items. This means that on this day, you will cut out all *dals, rajmah*, soyabeans, and so on and also milk, yoghurt and so on. The idea is not to go hungry, but to eat a controlled, healthy diet. If you want, you can have your *roti-sabzi* six times a day, but no *dals* and no dairy products, please.

You will also take all raw fruits, dry fruits and vegetables liberally. Please do not starve yourself; just eat what will keep you nourished without putting any sort of burden on the system.

Because of sheer habit, you may pine for various tasty items that you are used to eating, but exercise some self-control. It will yield dividends beyond your wildest imagination.

Eye exercises

Exercise No. 22:

Eyes also suffer due to lack of movement. A simple way to provide them relief is by shutting them and then tightening them hard. Hold for as long possible, loosen them but don't open them. Repeat at least 20 times. You can do this exercise whenever your eyes are tired because of too much of studies/watching television/driving or playing video games.

Exercise No. 23:
Look straight. Imagine that there is a huge X mark before your eyes. Move your eyes up towards the left and then bring it down to the right. Then look towards the top on the right side and towards the bottom on the left side. Do at least 20 repetitions on each side.

Exercise No. 24:
Imagine that are looking at the centre of a huge clock. Now rotate your eyes as if you are looking towards the hour 12 and then drawing huge circles. Make 20 eye rotations clockwise and 20 anti-clockwise.

Exercise No. 25:
Look towards the left shoulder and then towards right. Repeat 20 times on each side.

Exercise No. 26:
Look up and down 20 times each. Please ensure that your neck does not move.

Perfect Health in 20 weeks

Week 15

The previous Wednesday spent without eating lentils and dairy products has prepared your body for facing greater challenges. We will progressively move towards a mono-diet and finally reach the stage where we will ask our bodies to meet most of its energy demands from the calories that it has already stored so that it can flush out all toxins in the process.

You might have noticed that this is the first time that I have referred to calories, whereas this word is bandied about regularly wherever there is any talk about losing weight or repairing the body. People have a fascination for calculating calories.

The omission on my part was deliberate. You see, what most people do not know is that the calories from different items are as different as chalk and cheese. If all of them were similar, life would have been much easier for foodies. Supposing, they were allowed 2,000 calories a day. They would have taken 500 calories from *maida*, 500 from *khoya*, 500 from sugar and 500 from fat. They would have not exceeded the quota by even one calorie. Do you think they could have lived happily ever after?

In fact, why stop at these eatables? There are calories in tea and alcohol also. Can we make do with them?

The fact is that the four white snakes and some other items like them give us only empty calories, not nutrition. Now that you have thrown them out, we will benefit from the calorie calculations.

There was another reason why I was wary of referring to calories. There is no unanimity in the West on how many one should consume in a day. Every decade or so, they advise us to further cut the calorie intake. In fact, recently they have even started saying that a "starvation diet" is the best. Interestingly, what we in India had been recommending all along was earlier branded "starvation diet" by them, but is now coming into vogue.

In any case, we, in India need far fewer calories than people living in the cold-climate countries. For us, 1,000 calories per day is the subsistence level. If you are a sedentary worker, you can do very well with as few as 1,200 calories a day. If you are reasonably active (daily walk) then you can go up to 1,500 and if you do quite strenuous exercises, then you can handle even 1,800. Different items have different number of calories per gm. On an average, seven extra calories that we consume give us one gm of weight. This one gram or even 50 gm won't show on any weighing scale that we have at home. But if you start adding even 50 gm of weight a day, you may be one and a half kilogram heavier in one month and 18 kg in just one year.

That means that anyone who is one kilogram (1000 gm) overweight is carrying full 7,000 calories with him. These are enough to make him survive without eating anything for as long as seven days. Have you thought how many calories are in reserve with those who are 10 kg or 20 kg overweight? It is 70,000 calories and 140,000 calories, respectively.

Ironically, despite this huge store, we flare up even if our lunch or dinner is delayed by 10 minutes. "I am dying of hunger" is the common refrain. That is a not false alarm, either. That is actually how the body feels because it does not want to spend the stored calories. We do not intend to starve, either. By cutting down calories gradually, we are only training our body to make up the minor shortfall from extra weight that we are carrying.

All that we are doing is that we are eating 250 calories less every day by removing unhealthy items like sugar and also burning another 250 calories through exercise.

So, the total calorie reduction per day is 500 calories, which in a week would be 3,500 calories. As we mentioned, seven calories equal 1 gm. That means that in one week you can shed 500 gm (3500 divided by 7) without tears. Imagine, in 12 months you can pare 24 kg from your weight! Can there be an easier way of getting the hourglass figure that you always wanted?

So we proceed further on our calorie-cutting and disease-ending mission. This week, we unburden our system some more. You will cut out even *roti* and *sabzi*. Instead, you will be on *khichdi* and *dalia* (porridge) this coming Wednesday. In both, you should add vegetables liberally.

The *khichdi* will, of course, be made using the *dal* but the character of *dal* changes when it is cooked along with rice. As a result, while *chawal* and *dal* cooked separately may be slightly heavy, they are very easy on the system when made into *khichdi*. The same holds true of porridge.

It is needless to add that you should try to use porridge made from sprouted grains as far as possible. The vegetables you add to them will provide top-grade nutrition. Plus, you should also be eating raw fruits and vegetables, as in the previous week. Then there are juices too. If possible, go in for freshly extracted juices. If fresh juices are just not available, then you can also use the canned ones. Just make sure that they do not have added sugar in them.

So far, you have been adding Isabgol (psyllium husk) to your flour. But this Wednesday, you are not eating *chapattis* at all. So, you should take Isabgol with a glass of water at sleep time.

See how fresh you wake up the next morning! But a clarification is due here. You are passing through a cleansing process. Out of sheer habit, you will pine for items that you are used to consuming. So, at times you may feel uncomfortable, even miserable. This is only a passing phase. The real glow of health will come only later.

Another point calls for a clarification. Some well meaning but ignorant persons may advise you that one must keep on eating junk food because if you stop it, you will lose the habit and after that if you eat it, you will be violently ill. That is akin to saying that one must face a bullet every day. Who knows when someone may fire at you? Make no mistake. With practice you can learn to run faster, carry more weight or climb more stairs. But the capacity to eat cannot be increased by practice.

In fact, the discomfort that those who keep their system clean face, when they eat any undesirable item is a wonderful defence mechanism. It warns you that what you ate did not agree with you. Those who have ruined this early-warning system never get to know this and instead of unease they have to face a disease. So, it is better to be warned as soon as one eats something undesirable than to never know about it.

***

Now that your system is pretty clean, it is time to move on to *pranayam*, which is the art of utilising every breath fully and also take in as much *prana* from air as possible. That will send your vital energy soaring.

Nine out of ten people take 16 breaths per minute and inhale half a litre of air in each breath. That makes it a total of eight litres of air per minute. However, our minimum requirement is about 12 litres. When you are walking or running, the requirement increases manifold. That is why many of us become breathless on even slightest exertion.

The shortfall takes place because we have gotten used to shallow breathing. Only upper parts of the lungs are filled while the lower parts remain unused. Now the time has come to follow the yogis and reduce the number of breaths per minute to about eight but take in as many as four litres per breath, making it a total of about 32 litres per minute.

This form of breathing, which is called abdominal breathing or diaphragmatic breathing, is not peculiar to yogis. Every infant breathes this way. In fact, some mothers get worried that their child makes a big belly while breathing. There is no cause for concern at all. Rather, that is the right way to breathe and all of us should do exactly the same. Perhaps that is why it is said that a child is god-like. What a pity that we forget to do so when we grow up.

Now re-train yourself to breathe like a child. When you inhale, do so deeply while expanding your belly like a balloon. When you have taken in the maximum air, hold for a few seconds so that the air reaches every cell of the body. Then breathe out slowly and steadily so that every trace of carbon dioxide can be expelled. While doing so, you will also be contracting your belly.

Actually, you are not pushing breath into your belly. All that you are doing by making a big belly is allowing the diaphragm to be pushed downwards so that the lungs can fill fully. This way, you can take in your full quota of air.

Many people do exactly the opposite. They contract the belly when breathing in and expand it when breathing out. Please check yourself if you are one of those who make such a mistake.

Others have accumulated so much fat around their waist that they just cannot move their belly. But keep at it. Soon you will get the hang of it.

Begin with deep breathing for five minutes each in morning, evening and night. You should gradually increase it to three sessions of 20 minutes each. Also, whenever you find a minute to spare, breathe this way. May be you are stuck at the traffic light. Instead of fidgeting, why not put the time to good use? No one except you yourself will notice what you are doing.

Actually, you should be breathing this way all the 24 hours, but even these few minutes of conscious breathing will suffice to begin with.

Gradually you will become so used to this type of breathing that you will start taking every breath properly without you even noticing it.

It is a strange feature of our body that even when we misuse it in some way, it starts feeling comfortable in that misery. We all know that we must sit with our backbone straight. But most of us sit with the back curved. Try sitting straight and the back starts hurting. In the same way, deep breathing may initially leave you breathless. Don't let that scare you. Your body is only trying to adapt to the new technique.

Lack of air leads to lack of *prana* and that makes us touchy and irritable. Minor matters will upset you easily. Whenever you are feeling low, angry or sad, immediately try to get away from that place, lie down if possible and try to indulge in deep breathing for at least 20 minutes. When you get up, you will find that you have regained much of your composure and are better prepared to face the situation.

It is only desirable to lie down while doing so but not compulsory. You can also practise while sitting and even standing. Just train yourself to take your full quota of free oxygen.

Arm exercises

Exercise No. 27:
This week, we will add some exercises for the arm to your repertoire. Raise your hands forward at shoulder height and make them face each other. Twist your arms as if somebody is trying to break them. Then twist in the other direction. Do so 40 times in all.

Exercise No. 28:

Put both hands forward and make the fingers point towards the sky as if you are pushing against a wall. Pull the fingers towards yourself and feel the stretch in both palms. Make a tight fist. Open the fist and stretch the fingers towards you again. Do so 40 times in all.

Exercise No. 29:

As in Exercise No. 28, put both hands forward and make the fingers point towards the sky as if you are pushing against a wall. Now make the fingers move downwards as if you are beckoning someone to come towards you. Repeat this motion 40 times.

Week 16

It is time to take your cleaning operation a notch higher. This Wednesday, you will do some real fasting. As usual, there will be fruits, vegetables, dry fruits and juices aplenty. But as far as cooked items are concerned, you will be only on soup. This is the occasion that we were waiting for to give some genuine rest to the system for recovery and repair.

Mind you, we are not talking about the soup of the kind that they sell in markets, loaded with cornflour and condiments. Our soup will be a clear one, made out of vegetables. Normally, when we make soup, we mash the vegetables that we put into it and even sieve them. But since we are so used to munching something when you are eating normally, you should not mash the vegetables on this special day. You will get some satisfaction eating the small pieces of vegetables. Basically, you will be spending the day with vegetables boiled in lots of water with a sprinkling of salt and pepper.

It will be tough going as long as it lasts, but once you are through it, you will feel as if you have removed tonnes of weight from your system. As far as possible, try to bear the hunger pangs. But it has been noticed in some people that they become almost uncontrollable around 4 pm and 11 pm. If you are one of such unfortunate ones, indulge in a bit of *khichdi* or *dalia* but nothing more than that.

While this limitation of food becomes a weekly practice for you, we will also handle a very common problem this week. It is cough and cold. It has become so prevalent that people do not even go to a doctor when they cough and sneeze. There are so many remedies available over the counter that people either take them from the chemist or even remember them themselves. They think that it is very natural to have cough and cold during change of season. In fact, it has become so commonplace that people even do not count it as an ailment. "Oh, it's nothing, just some cough and cold," is the common refrain. Rather, it is known as the "common cold".

Actually, it is a warning sign that you have been overburdening your system by disobeying the laws of nature. As we will explain in the following paragraphs, there are certain set rules about avoiding a few foods at certain times, but we tend to ignore them. If you are prone to catching cold easily, you should read the following paragraphs very carefully and act on the advice religiously. If you do, I can assure you that you will contract cough and cold *only when you are keen to do so*. Give a fair trial to the do's and don'ts for a few months and you will be amazed at the results.

The problem with cough and cold is that although it is considered a minor disease, it tends to make your life miserable. You cannot work properly; you cannot think properly. And as it becomes chronic, you start having headache, sinus and sundry other complications.

1. **Never consume yoghurt (curds), *lassi* or other products made from yoghurt (like, *raita*) after sunset:** Do not ask me how it happens, but it is a fact that yoghurt when eaten after sunset tends to increase phlegm. The effect may be minor in some but serious in others. In Indian medicine system, human beings are divided into three types of constitutions:

    1. *Kapha,*
    2. *Vata* and
    3 *Pitta*

The first are prone to catching cough and cold easily. The second are the kind who can suffer from joint pains and so on often while the third have digestion-related problems aplenty. If you happen to belong to the first category, you will catch cold within days of eating *dahi* or drinking *lassi* at night-time. Since we do not know the relationship, we eat and drink such things on a regular basis spoiling our throat for life. Even if one is not of *Kapha* constitution to begin with, one develops the tendency by regular use of yoghurt at night after some years. So avoid it at all costs during the night.

2. **If you consume the aforementioned food items during the day, add salt and pepper to them before eating them:** Salt and pepper reduce the tendency of yoghurt to cause mucous formation. Those, who are prone to cough and cold, must make it a habit to add these essential ingredients, even during the daytime. You can also add *jeera, pudina, ajwain* and so on for taste's sake. But salt and pepper are totally unavoidable.

There is an interesting story related to this characteristic of yoghurt. A doctor after returning from the clinic was having his dinner in the rear courtyard. His wife was making fresh *chapattis* and bringing them to him hot.

She brought one, he savoured it and said: "Say, you have been asking for a diamond necklace for many years. I will get you one soon."

She was pleased that her cooking had melted her husband. So she cooked an even better *chapatti*. He ate this one and said: "I am sorry but I will only be able to buy you ear rings."

She was flummoxed that the *chapatti* had not shown the effect that she expected. So she worked extra hard on the next one. However, this time the husband said: "Forget it; I won't be buying you anything at all this year."

Naturally, she was in tears and asked him what had spoiled his mood. He said he would tell her later at night. When it was sleep time, she again confronted him. He replied: "It had nothing to do with your cooking. Just as I was having dinner in the courtyard, our neighbour, too, was doing so in his courtyard and I could overhear everything that he was saying to his wife."

"He asked her to bring a bowl of curd for him. I knew that eating this at night-time would cause him major complications. He had no choice but to come to me and I would be able to buy a necklace for you."

"He then told her to put some salt and pepper in it. I knew that this will help but since it is night-time, he will still fall ill but less severely. So I told you that I would only be able to buy earrings for you."

"He again told her that his throat was misbehaving and he would rather not have the curd. I knew that we would not be able to buy any ornament at all."

This story may be apocryphal but the effect of curd is a harsh reality. Give it up during night-time.

3. **Stop eating pickles, sauces and ketchups during the night:** These sour items too play havoc with your throat. Avoid them like the plague.

4. **Do not consume any food product whose temperature is below the room temperature at night:** The ice cream and the cold juices that you have at dinnertime are guaranteed to damage your throat. Even cold water can be a villain. Stop them henceforth.

5. **Do not consume hot and cold food products at the same time:** They not only ruin your teeth, they are also very damaging for your throat. Since we are ignorant, we routinely take piping hot pizza with chilled cold drinks. Why, in India we have also developed the habit of having hot *gulabjamuns* with ice cream. The result? Cough and cold are our constant companions. Leave

this tasty but dangerous pastime forever if you want a cold-free life.

6. **Do not drink water while eating any food product that is oily or greasy:** I know very well you have stopped eating such items, but if somebody in the family does and drinks water along with them, he is going to be in trouble. So, persuade him that oily food and water do not go together. If at all he has to drink something, he should take tea or plain hot water. Any cold item, be it milk or a cola drink, will be equally bad.

7. **Do not drink water with any oily nuts:** Be it groundnuts or pistachios; do not take water with them. That will make your throat very sensitive and sooner or later you will become prone to succumbing to cold. Groundnuts are particularly risky. So are items made-up of groundnuts and *til* (for instance, *gajak* and *revari*).

8. **Keep your head and chest properly covered in the cold weather:** If you are the kind who catches cold easily, you should keep your head covered when going out in cold weather. Even during summers, when you are going to sleep in an air-conditioned room, make sure that you are not in your vest. Instead, your chest must be properly covered.

9. **Be gargle-friendly:** Suppose you end up eating something which you should not have – may be a hot item along with a cold item. You will notice by the end of the meal that your throat has started misbehaving slightly. Do not wait. Immediately, do gargles with warm saline water. The sooner you do it, the better it will be. Another precaution you can take is that the last morsel of the meal should be taken raw, without any *dal* or *sabzi*. Also taking a few sips of hot water after a meal saves you from throat trouble. It is also good for your heart.

10. **Put a few drops of almond or mustard oil in your nostrils:** A few

drops of oil or ghee in each nostril at bedtime does wonders. Make it a regular habit. In fact, those who have interest in yoga must learn *jal-neti* and *sutra-neti*. Both these help in keeping throat trouble at bay.

More arm exercises

Exercise No. 30:
Raise your arms in front of you, with fingers pointing in front. Turn the fingers of both hands towards the left and then towards the right. Make 40 repetitions in all.

Exercise No. 31:
Make a tight fist in such a way that the fingers cover the thumb. Make big circles with the fists, 20 in clockwise direction and 20 in anticlockwise direction.

Exercise No. 32:

Grab your left wrist with the right hand and the right wrist with the left hand. Raise both hands above the head. If possible, try to take the clasped hands behind the head. Now try to pull both hands towards the left first and then towards the right. Make 40 repetitions in all.

Week 17

This is the week when for one day, you will go on a full-fledged fruit diet. The only cooked item you took last Wednesday was soup. You will give up that too this Wednesday and spend the day on fruits, vegetables and juices. By now, your body is well prepared to handle this situation without feeling deprived.

You might feel uncomfortable and pine for some hot food at times but please resist the temptation. It will only be false craving. Load yourself with fruits whenever the urge strikes. Please remind yourself that for thousands of years, human beings lived on fruits and vegetables without any cooked food at all.

Keep a gap of at least two hours between eating the fruits and vegetables. Supposing you had a breakfast of fruits at 8 am, have vegetables (carrots, tomatoes etc) only after 10 am. The next intake of fruits would be at 12 noon and so on and so forth.

There should be a similar gap between the consumption of fruit juices and vegetable juices too.

And as usual, you will be taking *Isabgol* at bedtime with a glass of water.

A note of caution is in order here. Fruits have the admirable quality to flush out residual waste material that has accumulated in the system over the years. So when you live exclusively on them for 24 hours, you will feel that you are having loose motions. Actually, it is the much-needed cleansing that is taking place. You will be fine after some time. However, you have to make sure that the fruits are properly washed because excessive spraying of insecticides and pesticides may have contaminated them.

Here, let me tell you about another interesting facet of nature cure. Whenever we eat something undesirable, our system considers it as a burden and wants to flush it out as soon as possible lest it causes any damage. You must have noticed that when you ate junk food for several days – for example when you went out for a wedding – you ended up having loose motions.

The system is in its way trying to tell you, "Look buddy, you ate something that you should not have. Now let's get it out. I am shifting to flush-out mode. All that you are to do is: one, not to eat anything solid at all for the next 12 hours or so, so that I can concentrate on the job at hand and, two, provide me with sufficient quantity of water and essential nutrients so that you do not get dehydrated and fall short of essential minerals."

If we go along with what it is suggesting, we can escape the ill effects of undesirable eating. But what do we actually do? We panic that we have had "food poisoning" and immediately take medicines to "cure" the loose motions. The wonderful rescue operation that Nature was launching for our sake is nipped in the bud. You escape the discomfort of loose motions but end up contracting a hundred other, far more serious, complications.

In a way, it was indeed "food poisoning." The *ghee, maida, khoya* and sugar that you had enjoyed at the party were veritable poisons. But to save you from them, the way out was through loose motions, not through medicines.

Next time you have such a "problem", thank Nature for such a wonderful defence mechanism. Suffer the inconvenience for a day or two and you would have atoned for your dietary sins, there and then. But if you take medicines for stopping the loose motions, you will be bottling up the poison inside you and will have to pay a heavy price for this. What could have been just one or two days of inconvenience will get converted into years of misery.

So, whenever you have loose motions, take it as a blessing in disguise. Give up on solid foods for about 12 hours. Live instead on liquid items like soup, juices, lemonade and so on. If nothing else is available, just take small sips of water from a glass in which you have added either glucose or one spoon of sugar and a pinch of salt (when you are having watery motions, you are allowed to take some sugar to replenish the loss of nutrients). You can take one glass of such water every hour. The sugar-salt-water solution, as you know, is called oral rehydration solution (ORS) and protects against dehydration, especially among children. That is all the diet that you actually need.

If the frequency is excessive, two side-effects take place. One, the patient feels weak. Two, there may be pain in the anal region. To avoid the first, make it a point to lie down and rest for a while after every visit to the toilet. And to protect against the pain, rub a bit of oil in the anal region before defecation.

Within 16 hours or so, you will be back to normal. If the motions still continue, you can take *dahi* (of course with salt and pepper) in which one spoon of *Isabgol* has been mixed. This will help control the motions.

If they have not stopped after even 24 hours, just chew a few tender leaves of *Peepal* or guava and you will be fine. If you try to stop the flow prematurely, you will have long-term complications like constant headache.

You need to take any medicine only if the loose motions don't stop after even 36 hours or so. Even then, go for the mildest one.

We move on to the next topic of the week, which is proper sleep. As we mentioned in a previous chapter, we need six to eight hours of sleep every day. If we sleep more than this, it means that there is something wrong with our body.

But the bigger malady is the attempt by some to cut down on sleep. When every minute means more money or a move up the social scale, some think that it is foolish to spend time sleeping. Nothing could be further from the truth. The right duration of sleep is an absolute must for recharging and recouping. One should not try to cut it down any further than six hours. Your performance will start deteriorating sooner or later if you do not take sufficient sleep. There will be physical ailments as well.

Some just cannot seem to fall asleep. If this happens only once in a blue moon, it is quite understandable. Stress, anxiety, excitement and so on, can disturb the sleep pattern. But if you have sleepless nights every week, or even oftener, then it is a matter of serious concern.

In any case, what time you fall asleep is also very important. Those who keep late hours are going against their body clock and may have to pay for this indiscretion. As far as possible, try to go to bed well before midnight, so that you can get up refreshed by 5 or 5.30. Remember, these six hours of sleep are far healthier than six hours of sleep from say 2 am to 8 am.

Lights-out time should be well-defined. A fixed sleeping time conditions your mind to shut down at a particular time every day. Also, use your bed only for sleeping and not for anything else (for example, reading). If you develop that habit, just going to the bed will send a strong signal to the brain that you must fall asleep.

On days when you just cannot fall asleep, forget about counting sheep. Instead, convert the waiting time into an ideal meditation exercise. Lie down in the bed with lights switched off, be aware of your whole body and then bring your attention to your breathing. Notice the rise and fall of the stomach. Move the attention up and down.

Now focus attention on your navel and notice its rise and fall along with the breathing. Recite a *mantra* or *shloka* for a few seconds. After that, concentrate on the sensations being felt around the navel. Just keep the attention there. Soon enough, you will be fast asleep.

Mind you, good sleep does not mean snoring. In fact, snoring is a very dangerous habit. There are cases where snorers choked and landed in serious trouble.

***

Catching those 40 winks during the afternoon is also very important. That will make sure that you are not out-of-sorts later in the evening.

Our next stop is right breathing. For the past two weeks, you have been trying out abdominal breathing. It must have become second nature and you won't even have to make a conscious effort because every breath automatically will be long and deep. Now we will benefit from the science of breathing from different nostrils.

You must have noticed that we breathe better from either left or right nostril at different times of the day. Breathing from a particular nostril has different effect on our psyche. Breathing in from the left and breathing out from the right gives us rest, calmness, power to introspect and reflect. Breathing in from the right and breathing out from the left provides energy, strength and agility. The former is connected with night and the latter with day, and are called *Chandra-bhedi* and *Surya-bhedi pranayam*, respectively.

This week, you should practice the *Chandra-bhedi* breathing. Use your fingers and the thumb to control your nostrils so that you breathe in from the left nostril; hold for a few seconds and then breathe out from the right. Do the same thing again and again, at least 40 times. After that, simply close your eyes and watch sensations flowing through different parts of the body, especially your head. Let calming thoughts spread deep within.

Exercise No. 33:
Stand erect, with your hands to the side. Slowly rise on to your toes, while simultaneously raising your hands, till they come together above your head. Hold for as long as possible. Come down. Repeat at least 10 times.

Exercise No. 34:
Rise on your toes, while you raise your hands to shoulder height in front of you. Palms should be facing down. Now turn at your waist towards the left, while both your hands also turn to the left. Go as far as possible, stay there and then come back to the original position. Now twist hands and the waist towards the right as far as possible. That makes one set. Do 20 sets in all.

Exercise No. 35:

Stand erect. Stretch yourself upwards, as if you are pretending to be taller than you actually are. Raise your left hand up high so that your elbow almost touches your left ear. While in this erect form, press with your head towards the left while using your arm to stop the head from moving. Continue this friendly tussle between the head and the arm till you are tired. Now repeat the whole regimen towards the right. Do 10 repetitions in all.

You will notice that this exercise only works if you have stretched yourself upwards. You hardly get any benefit if you are standing casually and simply press the head against the raised arm.

Week 18

As we are coming to the climax of our healing process, you will be putting in your best to resolve the problems gathered over many decades. It may be tough going but it will pay remarkable dividends.

The present week will find you living on a perfect mono diet. Choose any one fruit and you will spend the coming Wednesday entirely on that; so choose carefully, whether it is papaya or mango. Eat them slowly, savouring their taste, texture, consistency and flavour. Since you will be voraciously hungry, you will discover many qualities about them, which you had never noticed before.

While the fruit keeps you well nourished, your system will be doing two very important tasks. One, it will be cleaning itself of all the toxins that have accumulated over the years, and two, it will be repairing itself also.

Mind you, it is a full-fledged operation. The only difference is that it is taking place at home. You don't feel very comfortable during an operation in the hospital, do you? The same way, there may be some unease during this "operation". Bear with it bravely. After all, you are paying for the excesses that you yourself committed on yourself, albeit, unknowingly. Once you are healed, you will thank yourself that you undertook the brave mission.

What goes in your favour is that you must be already feeling much lighter and more energetic than what you were when you started on this wonderful journey 18 weeks ago. So, the motivation level is going to be really high. The dividends are only going to increase in the days to come.

Since you are taking an unusually light and restricted diet, make sure that you do not go hungry. If you are, there are chances that you will end up craving for tasty bites. So, I don't mind if you take excess of papaya or mango or whatever is the fruit of the day. Just don't succumb to the temptation of all the dangerous things that others consume routinely.

Please also remember that your diet should be healthy on the other six days of the week also. By healthy, all that I mean is that keep away the four white poisons and have everything else in moderation.

Still, we ignore the simplest of precautions, with the result that we only exist, and do not live. The human body is so very strong that even if you corrode it with poisons like alcohol and cigarettes, it still lives on for 60 or 70 years. The quality of life is abysmal, but the quantity is sufficient. So we ignorantly keep on arguing that so and so 'enjoyed' all vices and still survived for 70 years. My friend, it is not only a question of how long you survived. What matters is what you achieved in that period, and how much pain, illness and trouble you kept away.

It has been estimated that the pain and expenditure that one suffers in the last three years of one's life is equal to the pain and expenditure gone through in all the rest of the life. Why make yourself so vulnerable at that sensitive time? Prepare for your old age with love and anticipation; not with dread and apprehension.

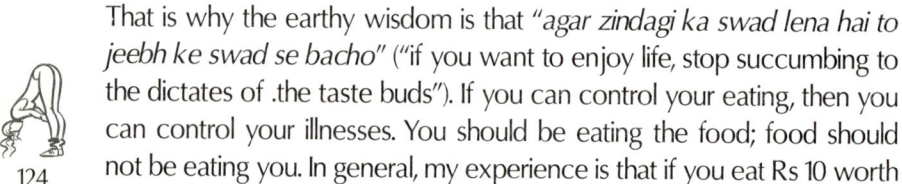

That is why the earthy wisdom is that *"agar zindagi ka swad lena hai to jeebh ke swad se bacho"* ("if you want to enjoy life, stop succumbing to the dictates of .the taste buds"). If you can control your eating, then you can control your illnesses. You should be eating the food; food should not be eating you. In general, my experience is that if you eat Rs 10 worth of junk food, you have to pay up 100 times as much (Rs 1,000) in terms of pain and medical bills. Surely, that is a terribly bad bargain.

If you have ever had a painful disease, you would have noticed that even one night is hard to spend. Even toothache can make your life so wretched that you cannot wait till the next morning. If you have money aplenty, I am sure you will be ready to spend Rs 10,000 to alleviate even one night of pain, right? So, if one night of your healthy life is worth Rs 10,000, please calculate how much you gain by leading one decade of healthy life that can be yours by following the advice given in this book. And why stop at one decade? The benefits can be for all the decades that you are going to have in future.

It is estimated that if you walk daily for 45 minutes for a decade, you have avoided one bypass surgery. Good bargain?

***

We have spent considerable time on improving the physical aspects of our life. You should be equally focussed on the emotional aspects. Our mood has a tremendous impact on our body. Even if you are eating healthy food, you will not be able to enjoy its full benefits if you do so under stress. That is why it is imperative to be in a positive frame of mind while taking your meals.

And, why only at mealtime? An optimistic attitude is a necessity round the clock. Bad food and lack of exercise are as much responsible for our poor health as are destructive thoughts like anger, revenge and jealousy.

What many do not know is that whenever we tighten our forehead and brows, our arteries and veins also get narrowed. That is the time when the blood supply gets obstructed. If the arteries are already narrow due to various deposits, it can lead to a heart attack or stroke.

Even if people around you are bad, you have to ignore their weaknesses for the simple reason that you want to save your own life. Brooding over anything is going to cause problems to us. So, make a cheerful disposition an integral part of your personality. You will live longer and better. Make it a daily habit to look for something positive in even the worst of the situations.

The breathing exercises that you have been doing will help. We take them a little further this week. We will concentrate on breathing in from the right nostril and breathing out from the left. Do it for at least five minutes at a time and see the results.

As mentioned earlier, the moon breathing (inhaling from the left nostril) is for calmness and rest while the sun breathing (inhaling from the right nostril) is for energy. Now that you have mastered both, you should practice the former at night-time and the latter at daytime. If you can do so at bedtime and wake-up time, better. The moon breathing will help you in having sound sleep. Practicing sun breathing when you get up will give a good energetic start to your day.

***

This week, I want to share with you the secrets of taking good care of your neck and back. Unfortunately, we treat them as springs and misuse them routinely till they start giving us pain.

The first secret is that you must move them in every direction that they are meant to be moved. Most of us keep our neck as well as the back bent forward most of the time. Aches are inevitable. So, whenever possible, bend your neck and back backwards, to counter the effect of forward slouch.

Secondly, while driving or sitting, our neck should not be hanging unsupported. Especially while driving, make sure that the back of your neck is in contact with the headrest. Even the back of your car seat should not be reclining more than 110 degrees.

The best way to ensure that your head remains in touch with the headrest is to adjust your rear-view mirrors – both inside and outside the car – while your head is pressed against the headrest. While driving, whenever you bend forward too much, you will not be able to see the rear-view mirrors and will be reminded of correcting your posture. What a pity that some of us even remove the headrests in the misconceived notion that it blocks the view.

Also, make it a point to take rest often.

Secondly, one should be very careful while lifting heavy weights. Never do so by bending your back. Always bend your knees instead and lift every object slowly. Those who have been leading a sedentary life should be particularly careful about this.

Another very important lifestyle change that you must bring about is to replace your soft bed with a hard one. Sleeping on extra-soft mattresses can play havoc with your back. You need not sleep on the bare floor, but at least your mattress should provide firm support.

Children who spend a long time reading or working on the computer (plus watching TV and playing video games) should remember the 10-10-10 formula. After every 10 minutes, remove your eyes from the book or the screen to look at something that is at least 10 feet away for at least 10 seconds. If it is some green tree in the distance, all the better.

Children instinctively take their eyes away from the books every now and then but since we are not fully aware of this necessity, we scold them for not concentrating on their study.

Actually, our eyes are designed to focus only on objects that are at least six metres away. But today we have to read as well as do other tasks that involve looking at things that are not even one metre away. That is why almost everyone has to wear reading glasses after the age of 45 or so. The only way to save our eyes is to give them rest often and look at things that are far away.

Even otherwise, being in natural surroundings, like near a hill, forest, river or forest gives us a sense of calm and peace. Whenever possible, break free from your daily routine and enjoy the natural elements.

We tend to copy the western culture, but only in terms of negative traits (for example junk food). They are much better off in some respects and we need to learn from them.

They work hard but then enjoy themselves well. On a weekend, it will be impossible to find anyone at home. They will pack their cars with picnic stuff, load cycles on to them and invariably, go into the wild. Those who can afford will have their boats in tow. And here we are: a family outing is at best a once-a-year novelty.

In Chandigarh, where I live, I have seen shopkeepers sitting outside their shops even on Sundays, which are closed days, doing nothing better than playing cards. For God's sake, spare a thought for your families. Be exclusively for them on these holidays.

Weekly offs are not furloughs but are a necessity, if one has to unwind after five or six days of hard work. Enjoy every moment. Maintain a balance between your professional and personal life. Quality time spent in the company of your near and dear ones will help you to do better in your workplace.

As I have been pleading earlier, you should treat the time spent in eating slowly and exercising to be an essential constituent of your professional work. You will be spoiling your work if you skip exercises and gulp your food. All these simple things comprise what is called common sense. It is another matter that common sense is not very common.

***

It is exercise time again. We are on to the general body exercises:

Exercise No. 36:
Stand erect so that your hands are joined above your head. Now bend towards the left as much as possible. Rest. Repeat the bending towards the right. In this way make 20 repetitions.

Exercise No. 37:
Repeat Exercise no. 36, but ensure that you are up on your toes first.

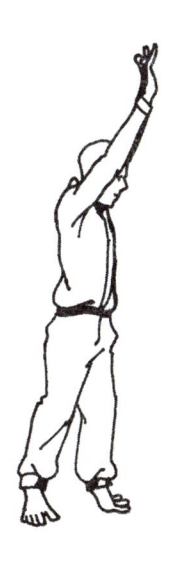

Exercise No. 38:
Go up on your toes as in Exercise no. 36, while your hands go towards the sky and the palms come together. Now twist towards the left, and then try to bend down and bring your hand towards your knees. Return to the original position and then repeat towards the right. That makes one set. Do 20 sets in all.

Week 19

This is the week of total and final cleansing of your body. On Wednesday, you will not take any solid food at all. From morning till night, it will be juices, juices and more juices. Please take care; it will be only fresh juices and not canned ones. All manufacturers claim that there are no added preservatives or sugar in their products. But tell me, have you ever eaten a fruit, which is quite as sweet as the juices they sell? So, get the juice extracted fresh in front of you.

Juices, like fruits and vegetables, act as natural laxatives. So, it will be advisable to drink them slowly. Even otherwise, we are by now used to taking juices in small sips.

One juice that is particularly laxative if taken repeatedly is that of sugarcane. Better avoid it on this particular day. Anything else will be just fine. *Mausambi* juice is especially good.

It will be a good idea to dilute your juice with water, up to 50 per cent. In other words, you can add half a glass of water to half a glass of juice and then drink it slowly.

Please make sure that you have such a glass at your usual breakfast, lunch and dinner time because it is then that you will be particularly hungry.

Hunger pangs will be particularly severe on this day but you have to ignore them somehow. It is only one day, after all. Please remember that your body has enough unused calories waiting to be disposed off.

Next day, you can have a bit of *khichdi* or *dalia*. Soon enough, you will find that you have got rid of many of your chronic diseases.

In fact, there are many people who remain on juice alone for several days. But that should be your personal choice. In normal cases, even one day of juice therapy is fairly effective.

Then, there are others who go a step further after having tested themselves on juice. They spend a day only on water, in each glass of which glucose or ORS (a spoon of sugar and a pinch of salt) has been added. But, you may do so only after you have gained enough confidence with drinking only juice.

If you keep this kind of fast once a week and eat sensibly on other days, you will well be on the way to perfect health. But those who find that their system is badly clogged do much more than that. Whenever you feel up to it, you can do a full nine-day therapy in the following way:

Day 1: Only water
Day 2: Juices
Day 3: Any single fruit
Day 4: All fruits
Day 5: Fruits and vegetables
Day 6: Soups (plus fruits, vegetables and juices)
Day 7: *Khichdi* and *dalia* (along with soups, fruits, vegetables and juices)
Day 8: *Chapatti* and *sabzi* (along with all other items used earlier like *khichdi, dalia*, soups, fruits and juices) (no *dals* or dairy products)
Day 9: Normal diet

Once you have done that and enjoyed the almost miraculous effects, you will be a convert for life. Most of my students do such therapy at every change of season – four times in a year. Rather, the senior ones go in for a longer-duration cleansing, which proceeds like this:

Day 1: *Chapattis* and *sabzi* (no *dals* or dairy products)
Day 2: *Khichdi* and *dalia*
Day 3: Soups (plus fruits, vegetables and juices)
Day 4: Fruits and vegetables
Day 5: All fruits (no vegetables)
Day 6: Any single fruit
Day 7: Juices
Day 8: Juices diluted with water
Day 9: Only water
Day 10: Juices diluted with water
Day 11: Juices
Day 12: Any single fruit
Day 13: All fruits (no vegetables)
Day 14: Fruits and vegetables
Day 15: Soups (plus fruits, vegetables and juices)
Day 16: *Khichdi* and *dalia*
Day 17: *Chapattis* and *sabzi* (no *dals* or dairy products)
Day 18: Normal food

As you can see, this kind of therapy is only for advanced students. But you cannot even imagine how many types of diseases can be cured with the help of this. After doing the course, it feels as if you have been running your body in first gear all your life and suddenly you have shifted to fifth gear.

So, choose for yourself how far you are willing to go. Even a day or two of light eating is good enough. After all, your digestive system also wants to take it easy once in a while.

***

Many of the modern youth suffer from outbreak of skin diseases. The cleansing that you have just done will take care of most of those problems. But you should, even otherwise, be more caring about your skin.

The greatest skin diseases are found in the people who take the most meticulous care of them. That had scientists surprised. After much research, it was found that washing the skin "properly" with soap was the culprit. You see, our sweat forms a protective layer against skin diseases. In our anxiety to be hygienic, we end up finishing this layer.

Soap is used mainly because we want to eliminate body odour. But bacteria causing body odour thrive only at a few places: in the underarms, pubic area and between the toes. The sweat everywhere else is water-soluble. So what you should do is that while bathing, use soap only at these three places. The rest of the body will be better off without the use of soap.

Soap should be particularly avoided on the face. Use only soap-free face wash.

For even better care of the skin, have a regular bath-time regimen. Before pouring water, dry massage your entire body with your hands. This should be done fairly briskly to get the blood circulation going.

Once you have poured water, again massage the entire body. Now is the time to apply soap to underarms, the inner thighs and between the toes. Please remember that the soap should not remain on the skin for too long. Wash it off quickly. The same holds true of shampoo also. Rinse it off within seconds of applying it. Some people keep it on for minutes, the same way as they do after oil massage. They perhaps think that keeping it there for long will make it more effective. Even the mildest soap and shampoo tend to be too harsh on the skin/hair.

After rinsing off the soap, again pat yourself dry. So, you have massaged yourself thrice – before pouring water, after pouring water and after rinsing off the soap and shampoo. Now is the time to use a towel.

This way, you will be able to maintain adequate hygiene and yet benefit from the antibacterial qualities of your sweat. Whenever you can, make the traditional face pack (*ubtan*) for the skin. Oatmeal, *besan*, rosewater, *malai*, turmeric, glycerine, *dahi*, lemon juice, amongst others are some of the usual ingredients. These will help you to keep the skin healthy and glowing.

It will also be a good idea to massage your body at least once a week. After applying oil, wait for at least one hour before taking a bath, so that the oil is fully absorbed.

For your hair, use the mildest shampoo. In fact, switching to baby shampoo is a good idea. And why shampoo at all? The traditional herbal powder made out of *amla*, *reetha* and *sheekakai* is so very hair-friendly. The only unwanted "side-effect" is that when you rinse it off, it messes up your bathroom. But one should be more concerned about the health of one's hair than the condition of one's bathroom.

***

Your breathing too will become subtler this week. You have already learnt *Chandra-bhedi pranayam* or moon breathing (inhaling from the left nostril) and the *Surya-bhedi pranayam* or sun breathing (inhaling from the right nostril). Now you will do them alternately. That means that you will take one moon breath and one sun breath and so on and so forth. This is called *anulom-vilom pranayam*. Doing so for as little as five minutes gives tremendous physical, emotional and spiritual benefits.

With practice, you will be able to increase the speed greatly. Regular practitioners can do it so fast that it becomes almost impossible to keep a count of how many breaths they took. But please do not try to hasten things right now. Take leisurely breaths and reap the benefits. It is very important to relax after completing the practice.

Another very good *pranayam* is *Kapalbhati* in which you do forceful breathing. But those who have high blood pressure should not try this out.

This week we will wrap up our exercise regime. You have now started to limber up every single joint of your body. The beauty is that if you are short of time, you can do lesser repetitions. In fact, one or two repetitions of each exercise can be done in five or seven minutes only.

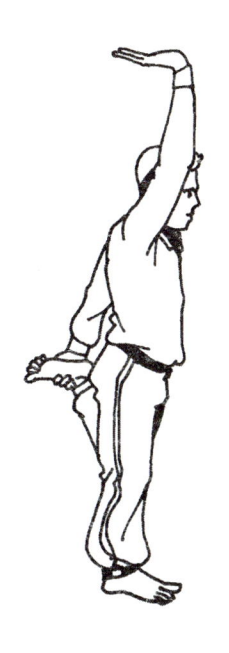

Exercise No. 39:

Stand erect. Bend your left leg. Hold your toes with your left hand and pull backwards so that your left heel is almost touching your left hip. Raise your right hand up. Stabilise yourself and try to look skywards. Stay in this position for as long as possible. Repeat the same exercise with the right leg and the right hand. Do 20 repetitions.

Exercise No. 40:

Stand erect. Raise your right hand. Bend forward slightly. Bend your left leg backwards as in Exercise no. 39 and grab your toes with the left hand. Pull back the leg as far as possible. Use the raised right hand to counter-balance and look towards the right palm. Hold for as long as possible. Repeat the whole exercise by switching the hand and the leg. Do 20 repetitions.

Exercise No. 41:

Stand erect. Hold your left ankle with the left hand and bend the left knee in such a way that it points sideways. At the same time, put your left sole on the right inner thigh. Now raise both arms above the head in *Namaskar mudra* while standing on the right leg. Hold for as long as possible. Repeat with the other hand and leg. Do 20 repetitions.

Exercise No. 42:

Instead of placing the left sole on the right inner thigh as in Exercise no. 41, place it in front of the right thigh. Then repeat the whole exercise by standing on the left leg and placing the right sole in front of the left thigh. Do 20 repetitions.

This brings us to the end of our exercise regime. Ideally, all these should be completed in the morning. But if you are short of time, you can do some in the morning, and some during the day. Please appreciate that as one's age goes past 25, there is bound to be a decline in one's strength, speed and stamina. But one thing that can be preserved till one's old age is flexibility. The exercises that you have done will help you in keeping all your limbs supple. The phrase is that "You are as young as your back is supple". Try to keep your body in fine trim with the help of these deceptively simple but highly effective exercises.

While these exercises are absolutely necessary to keep the body functional, you should strive to go even further. You must do some heavy exercises as well so that your heart and other vital organs remain in fine fettle. That is possible only if you do the exercises at such intensity that you become slightly breathless. In other words, your pulse rate should increase to optimum level.

There is a set formula to know how much your pulse rate, which is normally 60 to 72 beats per minute, should increase. Subtract your age from 220 and then find out 75 per cent (or three-fourths) of the remainder. That is how many times your heart should beat per minute after the exercise. For example, supposing you are 20 years old. Subtracting 20 from 220, you reach 200. Now you try to find out 75 per cent of that, which in this case will be 150. That means that your pulse rate per minute should increase to 150 after the exercise. The figure for a 40 year old will be 220-40=180 and 75 per cent of that is 135. So the 40-year-old man should confine himself to a heart beat of 135 per minute.

Once you have mastered the exercises, many of these can be done even in your office. For example, whenever you have been sitting for a long time, you can get up and bend from the waist left and right and front and back. Even that much of break will provide great relief.

Week 20

Taking one step at a time from one week to another, we have reached the stage where our body is as healthy and strong as Nature intended it to be. Very slowly and carefully, we have freed it from the clutches of every negative influence. With every passing day now, you will find yourself getting better and better. Now that the toxins that were causing you all the pain and diseases have been wiped out, the body will quickly repair itself and soon enough you will be back at your full potential.

You should realise that eating right is not only good for the body but also for the heart and the mind as well. It is also essential for your spiritual growth. The world's biggest seers are unanimous on that. Lord Mahavira says: "The biggest impediment in spiritual growth is wrong eating."

Similarly, Buddha says: "Inward calm cannot be maintained unless physical strength is constantly and intelligently replenished." Another of his famous quotations is: "Every human being is the author of his own health or disease."

So, if you are spiritually inclined, you will tread a smooth path to your elevation greatly by following the steps that have been described in the previous chapters.

While you have covered all physical aspects, it is equally important to be conscious of your mental health. Unfortunately, stress and tension have become an integral part of modern life. These cause as much harm to our health as physical factors.

Dissipating this stress is absolutely imperative if we have to lead a happy and peaceful life. Left unattended, it keeps on accumulating, till we reach a stage where we are angry or dissatisfied almost perpetually.

Suppose you are asked to lift a small glass weighing 50 gm or 100 gm. It is so light that there should be no difficulty at all in picking it up for anyone. But if you are asked to carry it for two or three hours, you will start feeling that it is the heaviest thing in the world. In the same way, when you carry a grouse for too long, it weighs heavily on your mind and troubles you immensely.

That is where the power of meditation comes into the picture. While its influences are multi-dimensional, lessening the tension is one of the millions of benefits that accrue from it. We will finish this book with a simple meditation, which everyone can do freely every day. As you will see, it is not connected with any particular religion. Nor does it use any holy word, *mantra* or *shloka*. So one can do it, to whichever faith one belongs to

You may like to record the script in your own voice or in the voice of some dear one. Please leave enough gaps in places where the asterisks have been put so that you can reap the full benefits. You see, meditation in Hindi is called *Dhyana*, which is *mindful awareness*. Just to be conscious of your thoughts can be very soothing.

It is human nature that we are rarely in the present moment. Either we are indulging in a reverie about the past or we are worried about the future. Secondly, we are not at the present place. We may be thinking of something, which is way beyond where we are. The meditation will teach you to be *here and now* and that too within your body.

This is the script:

Remove any metal or leather object that you may be wearing. Lie on the ground comfortably. Close your eyes slowly.

If you are used to keeping a pillow when you go to sleep, use it, by all means. But it would be better, if you don't use any pillow.

If you are wearing any tight-fitting clothes, now is the time to loosen them.

Let your legs be about one and a half feet apart, so that your thighs do not touch each other.

Your arms should be near your waist, about one foot away from the torso so that your arms do not touch the body. Palms should be facing upwards.

Be conscious of your breathing. Inhale deeply, exhale deeply. Try to relax yourself more and more with every breath.

If you have a deity, bring His image in your mind and seek His blessings. Now bring the images of your mother, father and any respected elder in your mind's eye and seek their blessings. Bring the image of your guru in the mind's eye and seek his blessings.

Take your attention to the toes of your left foot and be conscious of them. Just be aware where your big toe and other toes are. Notice their shape, where the nails are and where the skin is. If possible, be aware of the flow of blood in them.

Now tighten the toes as much as possible till they almost start hurting. Hold the tension . . . hold it a little longer . . . hold it some more and now all of a sudden let go. Release the tension entirely. Notice how toes feel now. Now observe your left foot with your mind's eye. Tense up your foot from toes to the heel as much as you can. Hold. Hold . . . Hold some more. Now let go. Notice how the foot feels.

***

- Now tense your right foot from the toes to the heel.
- Hold the tension.
- Hold some more.
- And now release the tension completely.
- Observe how the right foot feels.
- Now tense the right leg from the toes up to the knee. Increase the tension to the maximum extent possible.
- Hold the tension.
- Hold some more till it becomes impossible to hold it.
- Now let go completely.
- Observe the onrush of the blood.
- Observe how the leg feels.
- Now tense up the entire right leg.
- Hold the tension.
- Hold some more.
- Let go completely.
- Observe the onrush of blood. Observe how the leg feels.
- Compare it with your left leg.
- In your mind's eye, notice if there is any difference in the weight of the two legs?
- Any difference in the colour of the two legs?
- Any difference in the flow of blood in the two legs?
- Be totally focussed on your legs and nothing else.

***

- Now take the attention to the toes of your right leg and observe them minutely.
- Tense up the right toes.
- Hold the tension.
- Hold some more.
- When the tension becomes unbearable.

- Release it suddenly and completely.
- Observe what is happening to the toes.
- Be observant of even the slightest sensations.
- Tense the right leg from the toes up to the heels.
- Hold the tension.
- Hold some more.
- Release the tension.
- Observe all that is happening to the foot.
- Now tense the right leg from the toes up to the knee.
- Hold the tension.
- Hold the tension a little longer.
- Let go. Let go completely.
- Be focused entirely on the region between the toes and the knee.
- Notice each and everything.
- Now tense the entire right leg, from the toes to the groin.
- Hold the tension.
- Continue holding.
- Now release the tension completely.
- Keep focussed on the sensations.
- Focus on both legs.
- Compare the legs with the upper torso.
- Do you notice any difference in the weight of these two parts?
- Colour?
- Blood flow?

**

- Now include even your abdomen in the parts being tensed. In other words, tense every part from the toes to the abdomen. This is going to be more difficult than tensing other parts because most of us keep our abdomen tensed even otherwise.
- Hold the tension.
- Hold a little longer.
- Now let go.

- Remain very, very observant about whatever is happening.
- Don't anticipate anything. Just enjoy and observe whatever is happening.

**

- This time, include the chest also in the parts to be tensed. Tighten up every body part from the toes to the shoulders.
- Hold the tension.
- Hold on.
- Let go completely.
- Watch yourself.

**

- Take your attention to the fingers and the thumb of the left hand.
- Be totally absorbed in the fingers and the thumb. Observe every single sensation arising in them. Now tense your fingers, thumb and the palm. Make them as hard as stone.
- Hold the tension.
- Hold a little longer.
- Now let go.
- As usual, observe whatever is happening.
- Now tense the left fingers up to the elbow.
- Hold the tension for as long as you can and then let go.
- Observe all the sensations.
- Tense the entire left arm.
- Hold the tension.
- Hold a little longer.
- Now let go completely.
- Compare with your right arm.
- Notice even the slightest difference in the colour, weight and blood flow of the two arms.
- Focus your mind's eye on the right hand's fingers, thumb and palm.

- Tense them.
- Hold the tension.
- Hold a little longer.
- Now let go.
- Tense from fingertips up to the right elbow.
- Hold the tension.
- Keep on holding.
- Now let go.
- Observe everything happening there.
- Tense the entire right arm.
- Hold the tension.
- Hold a little longer.
- Now release all the tension.
- Just observe the right arm.
- Now tense up every body part from toes to the shoulders, including the two arms.
- Hold the tension.
- Hold the tension a little longer.
- Let go.
- Just observe yourself.
- Now tense every part from toes to the neck.
- Hold the tension.
- Hold it a little longer.
- Release the tension completely.
- Watch yourself.

**

- This time, tense your entire body.
- Give it your best shot. Try to increase the tension some more.
- Hold the tension.
- Hold some more.
- Let go. Let go completely.
- Just watch yourself.
- Once again, tense your whole body.

- Hold the tension.
- Hold a little longer.
- Let go.
- Watch yourself carefully.
- Now, for the third and final time, tense your entire body. Take care that no body part is without the maximum tension.
- Hold the tension.
- Hold for as long as possible.
- Let go. Let go completely.
- Be totally tension free and observe yourself.
- Be in the present moment. Be inside your body.
- Keep flitting from one body part to another and watch the flow of sensations.
- Remain in this state for as long as comfortable.
- Concentrate on your forehead and observe what is happening.
- Maintain this mindful awareness.
- When you want, move your fingers and toes very slightly to snap out of your state of bliss.
- Turn towards your left.
- Without opening the eyes, get up with the help of your hands.
- Sit in a cross-legged posture.
- Bring the image of your deity in the mind's eye and say a silent *thanks* to Him.
- Bring the images of your mother, father and elders in the mind's eye and say a silent *thanks* to them.
- Bring the image of your guru in the mind's eye and say silent *thanks* to him.
- Bring the image of the guru again in the mind and say *thanks for being present with you* all this while.
- Rub your palms together as if trying to warm them up.
- Touch them to your eyes so that the fingers are on the forehead and the palms cover the eyes.
- Open the eyes in the darkness created by the palms. Shut them and bring the palms downwards to the navel, as if you are touching your God or your children.

- Again, rub your palms together as if trying to warm them up.
- Touch them to your eyes so that the fingers are on the forehead and the palms cover the eyes.
- Open the eyes in the darkness created by the palms. Shut them and bring the palms downwards to the navel, as if you are touching your God or your children.
- For the last time, rub your palms together as if trying to warm them up.
- Touch them to your eyes so that the fingers are on the forehead and the palms cover the eyes.
- Open the eyes in the darkness created by the palms. Shut them and bring the palms downwards to the navel, as if you are touching your God or your children.
- Place the palms in your lap. Gently open your eyes and be aware of your surroundings.
- For the next few minutes, do not talk loudly. Also do not indulge in any violent activity.

***

Just this much of simple practice will help you in shedding a lot of tension. You will be able to lead a far happier life.

Put the advice given in these short chapters to good use and gain physical, emotional, mental and spiritual health that is your birthright.

Keep growing better and better!!!!!